TORN EARTH

DESMOND AND **VERA DENTON**

Copyright © 2020 Desmond and Vera Denton

All rights reserved. No part of this book may be reproduced, stored, or transmitted by any means—whether auditory, graphic, mechanical, or electronic—without written permission of the author, except in the case of brief excerpts used in critical articles and reviews. Unauthorized reproduction of any part of this work is illegal and is punishable by law.

BIOGRAPHY

DESMOND DENTON

Desmond Denton is a film director and scriptwriter, who has garnered much acclaim for his filmwork. Desmond has received over 17 international awards, including best written script writer at Monaco International Film Festival, Best Produced at CIFF and Best Feature film at Apollo International Festival. Desmond has represented South Africa and the WGSA as an author at international markets including London Screenwriter international festival, Cannes film market and New York Story Expo, he was officially chosen as a Berlinale Talent and Mofilm commercial film director.

Desmond Denton hails from Cape Town, South Africa. Being immersed in this picturesque multicultural environment, Desmond has developed a strong interest in telling the stories of authentic characters put to a test by unique circumstances. Writing this book has been an exciting challenge for Desmond, who tried to merge research data on the historic event of an earthquake with his vision of what it could mean to the people of a small provincial town.

VERA DENTON

Desmond has brought this story to life with his creative partner and wife Vera Denton. Vera holds her Masters in linguistics from the prestigious Moscow State Linguistic University, post graduate in psychology and she has been involved in all the stages of the development of this book.

Desmond and Vera together spend their time dreaming up new stories, traveling, raising their children and renovating their home in the snowy forest of Frostburg. The Denton family has a big love for exploring history and culture. Together they have built homes in South Africa, Vietnam and the USA.

Keep in touch with Desmond and Vera via the web:
Website: www.desmonddenton.com
Facebook: https://www.facebook.com/filmdirectordesmonddenton/
Twitter: https://twitter.com/directordes

SPECIAL THANKS

This book is part of the "As die Aarde skeur" film project and we are sincerely grateful to everyone who has been involved in it.

It has been a privilege to work with Cobus van den Berg and Tim Theron, exploring the town of Tulbagh.

Thank you Karin Tomilson for being involved in the early stages of the short film scripting "As die Aarde skeur" and your meaningful insights into character development.

I want to thank incredible actors Amalia Uys, Daniah de Villiers, Armand Aucamp for supporting this project.

Special thanks to the creative filmmakers Stefan Bezuidenhout, Gray Kotze, Tian Theron, Melissa Knoesen, Lindi Heila Smit, Charyke Coetzee, Paul Steyn, who got involved at the research stages of the project.

Thank you Aleit Swanepoel (The Aleit Group) for your involvement.

Special thanks to Oakfield College students who conducted research into marketing opportunities of "As die Aarde skeur."

Local Tulbagh residents and business owners received us with open arms and contributed to the successful research for the book and the development of the film project.

These special people are Elzanne Cronje and Ria Cronje (the local project co-ordinators), Santie Greef (a Tulbagh resident), Rosette Jordaan (Theuniskraal Wine Estate, an artist and photographer and an earthquake witness), Phil Gerhard (catering and accommodation), Carol Collins (Readers Restaurant, Tulbagh Tourism Committee Member, catering and accommodation, Norman Collins (NC Photography, Tulbagh E-News), Susan Smuts (Marmalade Angel Studio), Sofia Joemat (Tulbagh Tourism Committee Member), Peter Nel (Fynbos Guest Farm, Nature Reserve and Animal Rehab, Jayson Augustyn-Clark (Cape Dutch Quarters, Museum Board, Church Street Committee.

We also want to thank Tulbagh Museum, Seeff and Wesgro with its representative Monica Rorvik who has been invaluable in bringing strong community development elements into the project.

Writing this book was made possible with the support of Glen Snyman and his organization PARC (People Against Race Classification) with a passion to unite people beyond their differences.

FOR GRACE DINGAAN, MY AMAKULU

Grace Dingaan, heartfelt thanks for all the time you invested in me. You were there since I opened my eyes to explore this world. You guided me with your kindness and your beautiful Xhosa songs hummed me to sleep when I was little. On your back you carried me while you were doing so many tasks. It was an honour to have you partake at our family celebrations, our weddings. I thank you for your gift, your time, your love, your amazing stories. You learnt Afrikaans in our house, but in fact taught us so much more. You kindled in me a true passion for stories by sharing yours. You are my family and I am blessed to be yours.

PROLOGUE

On the night of 29 September 1969 an earthquake registering a magnitude of 6.3 on the Richter's scale hit the small picturesque town of Tulbagh in the Western Cape, South Africa. In an area that is not prone to earthquakes, the ground shook, tore and left a prominent scar. A scar that was running unbroken through the town and leading right up to the church, where it stopped, leaving the worship building unharmed.

What is to unfold on these pages is the story inspired by real-life events. It does not carry real names and biographical events, but our subjective interpretation of them. When we started the research for writing this story, we were touched by the courage and perseverance of people in this area: the personal experiences of earthquake survivors, amidst a very tense time in South Africa. As we journey through the events that took place before, during and after the earthquake, we will witness the response of human nature to that of Mother Nature.

CONTENTS

PART ONE

1. Morning 3
2. Bells 11
3. Invitation 16
4. Streets 20
5. Church 24
6. Heist 29
7. Feast 39
8. Punishment 43
9. Sisters 47
10. Dinner 53

PART TWO

1. Tulbagh 59
2. Rats 64
3. Snakes 68
4. First Shakes 72
5. The End Of The World 76
6. Church Street 80
7. Pipes 83
8. Sugar And Candles 88
9. Door 95
10. River Of Lights 100

PART THREE

1. Aftermath 107
2. 29 September 2019 112

PART ONE

CHAPTER ONE

Morning

It is the 28th of September 1969. The night is dark, the air cold. The old farmhouse is quiet. The only audible sounds are those of the yellow wooden floors, creaking while exposed to the changing temperature, and the swinging of the pendulum of the vintage grandfather clock in the living room. To Marietjie it feels like an eternity before the sun will rise between the mountains. She is lying in bed with her brown wavy hair spread on the pillow and her deer eyes wide open. She has been struggling to sleep for quite some time now, often lying in bed anticipating daybreak so that she could busy herself with all that needs to happen in the van Schalkwyk family household.

The grandfather clock chimes. It is seven o clock. *Finally,* Marietjie thinks to herself as she gets out of the bed swiftly and walks to the window draped with Classical Victorian curtains. The cold darkness of the night is lifting as the early morning sun slowly reveals the valley. The shadows of the valley and mountains, made up of all hues of purple, are moving to make room for the new day. The rooster is waking the world with his loud triumphant chant.

In a farmworkers' house close by, Grace Dingaan is sitting at a candlelight, praying like every morning. She is the main housekeeper at the van Schalkwyk homestead. She has been with the family for the last 20 years and Marietjie has grown up under her care. She often calls Grace her umakhulu (grandmother). When Marietjie and her younger sister Jana were still little, Grace carried them on her back, tied with a blanket, while cooking, cleaning, washing dishes and hanging up the washing. Grace is now in her late 50's. She is a short Xhosa woman, with a gentle voice and hands that are not afraid of hard work. She can be strict and decisive if necessary, yet most of the time she is caring and loving.

Being the housekeeper, Grace has been part of the household and shared its memories, often filled with laughter and fun. She was also a witness to how the house grew quiet after the unexpected passing of Mrs. van Schalkwyk.

How quickly time flies, she thinks. She looks at the radio clock, a gift from the van Schalkwyk family, and hurries to get dressed, putting on her overcoat. She rushes out of the house into the freezing air outside. Grace leaves her own home early on a Sunday morning to take care of another home and the family she loves.

She unlocks the back door to enter the kitchen area of the van Schalkwyk house. The first member of the household to greet her is Daantjie, the house dog, his tail wagging with excitement. She shakes off the cold and as she closes the door, she gently pushes Daantjie aside and hurries to switch on the oven to preheat it to 180 degrees Celsius. The air slowly warms up in the kitchen.

Grace knows Daantjie's impatient temperament, so she feeds the dog first. She washes Daantjie's bowl, fills it with food and takes it outside to put it next to the bowl filled with water. She returns and washes her hands before opening the glass bowl covered with a damp cloth. She then takes the dough from the bowl and kneads it to form a large loaf of bread. She then adds ground coffee and water to the coffee pot to let it simmer on the stove. Mr. van Schalkwyk is fond of his coffee first thing in the morning. Marietjie, on the contrary, likes English tea, just like her mom used to.

Grace then puts the Piet Fluit kettle (whistling tea kettle) on the stove next to the coffee pot. She places an enamel mug for the father on the table and also a Bone China teacup with a saucer for Marietjie. While Grace is putting the bread in the oven, the Piet Fluit kettle starts to whistle. By then the kitchen is filled with sounds and smells, of which the aromas of freshly made coffee and warm bread are the most alluring.

Jana, the youngest daughter in the van Schalkwyk family, hears the sound of the Piet Fluit teapot from the kitchen. The sun rays are starting to beam into her window. She turns around, away from the sunlight and covers her face with a blanket, in an effort to sleep some more.

Marietjie, dressed up and ready for the day, enters Jana's room and says loudly, "It's time to wake up."

In response, Jana buries herself deeper into the blanket.

"We need to leave home earlier today, Jana. I want to visit the seamstress before church," Marietjie pronounces.

Jana groans loud enough to be heard from under the blanket.

"Jana, you really need to take your responsibilities more seriously!" says Marietjie annoyed.

No response from Jana.

"I expect you to get ready and come down for breakfast!" commands Marietjie and leaves the room closing the door with a bang.

Pieter, the father of the van Schalkwyk family, a tall man with deep brown eyes and big strong hands, walks into the kitchen, his hot coffee waiting on the table.

"Molo Grace (Morning Grace)," Pieter greets Grace in Xhosa.

"More Meneer (Morning Sir)," replies Grace in Afrikaans.

He sits down at the table and opens the freshly baked bread that Grace has wrapped in a cream white kitchen towel and served in a breadbasket.

"Enkosi Kakhulu (Thank you)," says Pieter and takes a large silver bread knife. As he is cutting the bread with the crunching sound of the breaking crust, steam comes out of the loaf. He takes another knife to spread butter and jam from traditional glass bowls and as he does so, the butter melts on a still-warm slice of bread.

Marietjie enters the dining area still frustrated by the conversation with Jana. She greets her father politely and sits down across from him. She adds a cube of sugar to her tea.

"Father, we need to go past the dressmaker before church today. She is busy with alterations," Marietjie says.

The father nods his head and takes a sip of coffee. It is quiet at the table as they sit without exchanging a word for some time.

In the meantime, Jana hears the gentle murmuring of Grace's voice as she enters her room. She is humming a Christian hymn, one Jana has heard many times over the years. She keeps her eyes closed, pretending to be sleeping. Grace is not discouraged at all by this and puts the plate with warm bread and jam on Jana's dressing table. Next to the plate she places a cup of warm milk sweetened with condensed milk. She then takes Jana's church clothing out of the cupboard and hangs it out, ready for her to jump into when ready. She leaves the room still humming.

After breakfast Marietjies' father leaves the house to talk to Isak, the foreman on the farm. Isak, a short man with brown skin and a bald head, is the third generation of his family that has worked for the van Schalkwyk family on the farm. His small farmworker house has a little garden yard, a plantation of pumpkins, onions, green beans, lettuce, and even roses. It is clear that Isak takes great effort to care for this garden and his house.

Little Sune, Isak's youngest daughter, comes out of the house. She is putting on her overcoat on the way and greets Mr. van Schalkwyk, "More Meneer (Morning Sir)."

Mr. van Schalkwyk nods his head in response.

Little Sune walks past them towards the van Schalkwyk homestead, excited for the new day. She helps out at the farmhouse, learning from Grace and takes great pride in it. Being nine and having responsibilities at the grand farmhouse makes her feel very mature. She loves being in this house, surrounded by the exquisite cutlery and dishes, elegant furniture and drapings, delicate bedding and clothes. At the house her chores include helping Grace with hard work like washing, cleaning, scrubbing, but she is being trained to take care of the whole house too. One day she wants to take care of the house like this on her own.

"Jana, aren't you dressed yet?" Marietjie enters Jana's room again. She notices the empty enamel cup and leftover bread crust on the plate. Jana remains under the blanket enjoying the warmth. "I do not have time for this now. Come now or I will drag you out of the room," says Marietjie still annoyed.

Jana responds equally frustrated, "I really do not want to go to this dress fitting again!" It is clear that Jana is not interested in playing the flower girl dress-up for Marietjie's upcoming wedding celebration.

"Jana, we have to do it before church. Father is waiting," Marietjie pleads. Marietjie and Jana seem to come from two different worlds, in both personality, and looks. Though both are beautiful, Marietjie has her father's long length, brown hair and eyes and Jana, well, she is short, her straight wiry hair is the color of straw, and her eyes blue, like her mother's.

The girls hear the honking of their father's car. Pieter van Schalkwyk is not a man of many words, but the honk says it all. Marietjie looks at Jana, mentally conveying the message, *you will be in trouble.*

Jana looks at Marietjie. "What? Being on time is being late?" Jana asks sarcastically, as she drags herself out of bed.

"You said it, not me," replies Marietjie.

The van Schalkwyk dwelling is surrounded by tall trees, bushes, and flower beds. Michael, a young boy from the local orphanage, is hiding between the bushes. He sees Marietjie coming out of the front door. She strides with confidence and a sense of purpose. The leaves hustle softly as Michael moves deeper into the bushes to avoid being seen. He holds his breath.

A few seconds after Marietjie, Jana rushes out, still a bit deurmekaar (flurried), trying to finish her hair as she walks. Michael has been waiting for Jana. Without leaving his hiding place, Michael sticks out a hand holding a piece of paper. Jana flinches in surprise and stops for a second to figure out what is going on. By now Jana knows Michael quite well, so she smiles, realizing that a new adventure is waiting. She quickly glances around to ensure that nobody sees her receiving the letter, and she carefully takes the piece of paper and hides it behind her back.

CHAPTER TWO

Bells

Much of the activities in town cease on a Sunday morning. The valley seems almost peaceful. The church bells echo through the empty town streets and beyond. Most shops are closed and people are going to church, as they are expected to. In the distance from the van Schalkwyk homestead, the farm workers and their kids, dressed up in their best attire go to church too. Grace, Isak and Sune are among them. On the fences along the dusty roads crawl hot pink Zimbabwean creepers and orange Cape honeysuckles. The church that farm workers go to is a small wooden building on top of the hill, it has no fancy ornaments or wall decorations. As the farm workers enter the church they join the rest of the people in songs. The church hymns can be heard over the hillsides. It is a pleasant melody, a melody that hides much of the daily struggle. The words of the song echo through the valley, "When peace like a river, attendeth my way, when sorrows like sea billows roll. Whatever my lot, Thou has taught me to know, it is well, it is well with my soul."

There is another church in the small town of Tulbagh. It is a tall stone building with its pointed roof and soaring lines. It is peering into the endless sky, far above attainment. Its bells are calling the people of Tulbagh and everyone can hear them, but not everyone can answer the call. The farm workers are not allowed in there, nor another group – the orphans. This is the church that the van Schalkwyk family will attend after their dressmakers' appointment.

The dressmaker is in her shop, waiting for the girls. She takes a look at the watch. She does not want to be late for church. She also does not want people to know that she works on Sunday either, so she has left the "*Closed*" sign on the door, to avoid gossip. When the seamstress hears the car, she opens the door. Marietjie and Jana enter, their father is waiting in the car. Inside the shop, there are mannequins with colorful dresses, all kinds of fashionable hats, shoes, and accessories. In the centre of the room, there is a mannequin with Marietjie's wedding dress on it. It is a rather conservative white dress with some lace inserts and long sleeves. Marietjie looks attentively at her dress, while the dressmaker is waiting for the verdict. Marietjie is studying the dress, looking for minor flaws, rather than taking in the whole picture. She finally says that she likes how the dress is taking shape and that she is ready for the fitting.

"That is wonderful," responds the dressmaker, and as soon as she has handed a small, flower girl dress to Jana, she starts taking down the wedding dress for Marietjie. Jana is not thrilled at the prospect of fitting, but she obeys and pulls the dress over her head in a careless manner.

As soon as Marietjie's dress is on, it becomes obvious that it needs quite a bit of adjustment to fit her figure.

"Oh, my meisiekind (girl), you have lost weight! I have told you before and I tell you now, it is not a good idea to try and lose weight before the wedding day! I cannot keep on taking it in endlessly," complains the seamstress.

"I have not tried to lose weight," replies Marietjie sadly.

"What is it then? Have you been sick?" asks the dressmaker.

Marietjie does not answer and simply looks away.

"Well then, try keeping this weight, or all our work is in vain," instructs the dressmaker while skillfully pinning the dress.

When the pinning is done, Marietjie looks at herself in the long shop mirrors. She stands very still, staring at her own reflection and allowing her thoughts to flow uninterrupted. She is well aware that she keeps on losing weight because she doesn't care about food anymore. She struggles to enjoy its taste.

She thinks how this dress fitting is supposed to be a happy event, full of excitement and joy, only for her it is not. She thinks that, if her mother were here with her, guiding her and sharing the experience, everything would feel different. If it was not for her mother's death…. Here Marietjie catches up with her train of thought and stops it full speed. She cannot go there again. She cannot afford to.. She takes a look at the time. .

Very little attention has been paid to Jana during this fitting. She is in her flower girl dress, feeling awkward in all the white frills and lace wrapped around her. The dress feels awfully uncomfortable and she thinks of the humiliating moment when she will go down the aisle throwing around the rose petals. *Is there any age limit to being a flower girl?* Jana remembers Marietjie mentioning that Jana is too young to be a bridesmaid. *What if I find a way to prove to Marietjie that eleven-year-olds are too old to be flower girls?* Jana looks at the finished dress and realizes that nothing could change the arrangement. People of Tulbagh expect Jana to be part of the wedding and Marietjie will make sure that this expectation is met.

How boring this whole wedding preparation is to me! Thinking of something better to do reminds Jana of Michael's letter. *Maybe I can read the letter right here in the shop, behind the dressing screen, while Marietjie is busy.* The letter Jana has received is nothing more than a piece of paper folded in three and glued together to resemble a closed envelope. On top of the letter, there is simply one word "*Jana*".

By the time Jana is tearing open the glued piece of paper, Marietjie is walking towards her and finds Jana behind the screen with a letter in her hand and a guilty expression on her face. This expression alone makes Marietjie come to the conclusion that the letter is compromising her sister's reputation, so Marietjie snatches the letter out of Jana's hands.

"Give it back!" exclaims Jana.

Marietjie tries to calm Jana down by saying, "Not right now. We will discuss it later."

Jana understands that she will not see the letter again and attacks Marietjie, "You are trying to control me, as if you are my mother, but you are not. You are nothing like her!"

After that Jana turns around and walks out of the dressmaker's shop banging the door.

Marietjie has not expected this to happen. Frankly, she doesn't even know why she has snatched the letter from Jana. It would be rude to read it. Throwing it away would make Jana mad. Marietjie has no intention to keep this letter either. So, what is she supposed to do with it and more importantly, what is she supposed to do with Jana who ran into the street in her Flower girl dress?

Lately, acting out has become a norm for Jana, just as pretending to be a strict parent, for Marietjie. Ever since their mother's death, father has been drawn back emotionally and Marietjie has been playing the role of a mother. To Marietjie's frustration it brought nothing but constant conflict.

CHAPTER THREE

Invitation

The bus rattles as it follows the curved roads up and down through the mountains and the beautiful landscape all around. Karla, a 23 year old girl, is sitting alone staring out of the window at a sight she has a very distant memory of.

She was born in the picturesque town, Tulbagh, and later moved with her parents to the Netherlands, where her father started his small tulip farm and a new life for his family. Karla was ten at the time and everything seemed different and strange in the new country. Vivid memories of Tulbagh and her fun childhood friends and familiar places filled her thoughts all the time. As it often happens, Karla idealised the past, forgetting the tears and unnecessary details. All those years she longed to return to Tulbagh oneday.

Karla's parents, however, did not share her enthusiasm. Mr. and Mrs. Coetzee often spoke about the regime of apartheid and told Karla that it was dangerous to separate people against their will. Her parents explained to her that they did not see a bright future for South Africa and that is why they had moved to the Netherlands, the country of their ancestors.

As time passed, Karla started to like a lot of things in the Netherlands. She made new friends, new places became familiar and even some Dutch foods became her new favourites. Yet, something deep in her heart did not change though. She still longed to return to her hometown of Tulbagh. She simply had the conviction that it was where she belonged.

In the years to come, her family never went back to visit South Africa, even though they had close family in Tulbagh. She was the one who diligently wrote letters to the relatives. That was her only way of getting a glimpse of what was going on in Tulbagh during those long thirteen years.

In one of the recent letters, her aunt shared the news that Marietjie van Schalkwyk was getting married that October. The name seemed familiar to Karla, so she pulled out an old photo album.

All the photos in the album were diligently glued in a chronological order and also had dates and names written underneath. Karla was looking for photos of Marietjie.. She spotted one of them, where Marietjie and herself were holding each other's hands and smiling broadly. Under the photo it stated: "*Karla and Marietjie, June 1953*". Then she found a photo that was signed as "*The van Schalkwyk family, September 1952*".

Karla compared the photo of Marietjie and the daughter of the van Schalkwyk family to confirm what she had guessed: Marietjie van Schalkwyk was indeed her old friend. At that very moment, an idea came to Karla's mind. If she managed to pull off a little trick, she could visit her hometown of Tulbagh.

The very next day she went to the calligraphy shop on the other side of town. When she entered the shop, where she hoped nobody would know her, she represented herself as Marietjie van Schalkwyk, who is soon to be married to Jacques van der Merwe.

Pretending to be Marietjie, she said that she wanted to order a sample card for her wedding invitations, "I need only a sampler now because I want my parents to agree with the design before we send it to all our friends."

She continued, "The invitation should read Marietjie van Schalkwyk and Jacques van der Merwe invite Karla Coetzee to their wedding, which will take place on October 11th, 1969, at 4 p.m. at the local church."

She wrote down the details and emphasized that, while they were still working on the choice of venue and church, the sample invitation should state strictly what she had written down. After that Karla looked through different designs, trying to choose one that would look more South

African. In just a few days she was in possession of a fake invitation to Marietjie's wedding.

She was somewhat concerned that her parents would see through her cunning plan, but when Karla told them that she had received a letter from her aunt with an invitation to the wedding of her childhood friend in South Africa, Mr. and Mrs. Coetzee were so surprised that they did not find any reason to refuse their daughter a visit to Tulbagh. They agreed that she could go under the condition that she would stay with their relatives.

Now, two months later, Karla is on the bus rapidly approaching the town of Tulbagh, she is finally coming home. *It feels like a lifetime ago,* she thinks to herself. The bus drives on the mountain pass and Karla can see her hometown in the beautiful valley below. She is overjoyed at the realisation of the one dream she had hidden in her heart all those years in the Netherlands

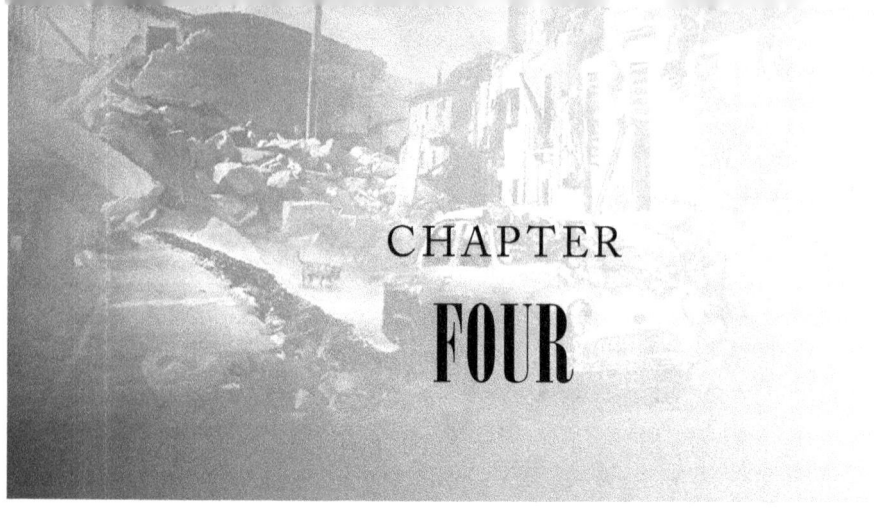

CHAPTER
FOUR

Streets

The bus has finally stopped. People on the bus, that have been motionless for the last hour, jump to their feet grabbing their belongings and rushing to the exit, as if late for an important appointment. Karla is not in a hurry. She tells herself that she is waiting for the scurrying of those leaving the bus to calm down. Truth is, she is taking some time to calm down her own emotions. This is the moment she has been waiting for for sò long.

In just a few minutes, the bus is empty. Karla is the last to leave the bus and take her bag from the luggage compartment. It is still early morning, but the sun is already bright. She closes her eyes and breathes in the fresh air, enjoying the smell of fynbos, a distinctive type of vegetation found in South Africa. She lets the sun shine warm upon her face. A few seconds later, the light morning breeze gives her a chill and she puts on a jersey over her short dress to cover her arms and back. Yet, she soon regrets doing this, as the heat intensifies. She removes the jersey again and remembers what her family used to say about the weather here, "It can be four seasons in one day in the Western Cape." She smiles, she is so glad and can hardly believe that she has finally arrived in Tulbagh.

She walks towards what appears to be one of the main streets in Tulbagh. She senses that it has a sleepy, otherworldly feel. The buildings show the history of both Dutch and British descendants that have settled in the area from the early 1800's. As she walks down the street with her bag, she is fascinated by how little has changed here over the years. This is the same street she remembers, the very street she knows so well. Only béing in this street feels so completely different.

The entire experience is so strange that she feels taken aback. It does not feel like coming home, but rather like sleepwalking in an odd dream. *How can everything look just as it used to and yet feel so different?* thinks Karla. *Has the atmosphere of the place really changed so much? Have I changed so much?*

It feels like seeing a ghost town! She can finally describe her experience in her own thoughts. She stops in the middle of the street and puts down the bag that suddenly weighs heavy. She feels confused and even a little bit lost. *Where am I supposed to go now?* She feels estranged and a loss of direction.

Looking around, she notices that she is standing close to a house that looks more familiar than others. She remembers seeing it in the photo with the happy van Schalkwyk family on the front porch. *This is Marietjie's house*, Karla figures out. As she is standing there staring at the house, she sees a young handsome man approaching the building and then knocking on the door. A maid opens, they talk for a few seconds, then he turns around and leaves; The door closes.

The young man notices Karla standing in the middle of the street. She is a beautiful young girl with blonde hair and a friendly smile. She is wearing a very fashionable short dress, that together with her traveling bag, immediately give away the fact that she is not from Tulbagh. The man is surprised to see someone new in this sleepy town. Karla, seeing the impression she has made, is smiling even broader.

"Excuse me, is this Marietjie's house?" she asks.

"Yes, it is," he answers.

"I need to introduce myself," Karla says confidently. "My name is Karla Coetzee. I used to live in Tulbagh with my family before we moved to the Netherlands. Now I am on my way to Ben and Truia Coetzee. They are my close relatives, but I do not remember where their house is."

She knows exactly where to go, but she does not want to miss the opportunity of talking to this young man.

"Welcome back," the young man says. "My name is Adriaan and I know where the Coetzee's stay. It is not far from here."

"Could you show me the way, please?" asks Karla.

"I could", responds Adriaan. "Can I carry the bag for you?"

"That would be nice of you," she smiles.

On the way, Karla and Adriaan chat about the Netherlands and South Africa, without him ever mentioning either Marietjie or the fact that they are engaged and soon to be married.

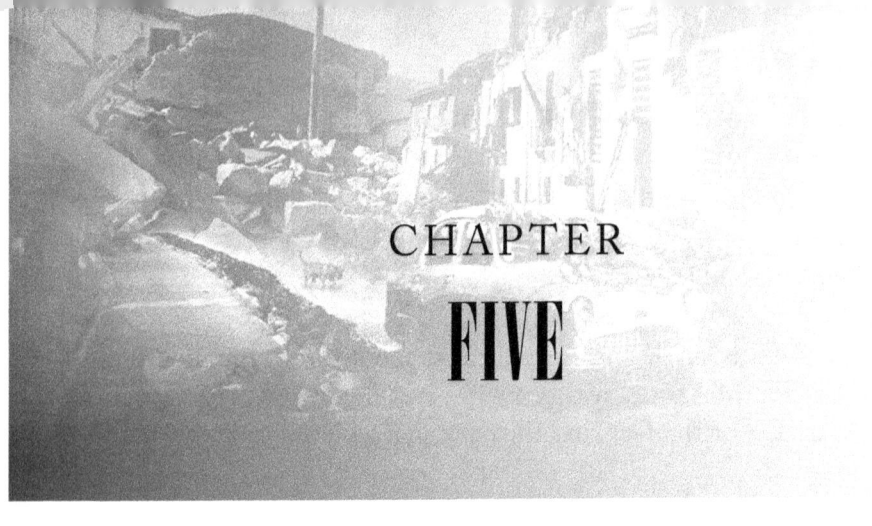

CHAPTER
FIVE

Church

The old church on top of the hill stands proud of its architecture. It is a beacon of hope to many, a place of coming together for some and a sign of exclusion for others. The church is built in the original cruciform shape. It has two galleries on the sides and one at the back. Beautiful stinkwood furniture and the thatched roof show that no detail has been spared in the pursuit of creating a proper place of worship.

The sound of the old organ welcomes the congregation, just like every other Sunday. People move to their usual seats, with their red songbooks waiting in the compartments in front of them. Parents have to keep their children quiet during services or face looks from others. This is how it happens every week with no or little difference. Everyone comes to show face, to pay tithes, doing what is expected of them in this small community.

Adriaan is sitting inside the church. He does not see his fiancee anywhere. Marietjie and her family usually come to the church early, but not today.

He made an attempt to visit Marietjie before church this morning, but Grace told him that Marietjie and Jana went for a dress fitting, something that according to the wedding tradition he should not know much about. Grace did assure him though that Marietjie and Jana were going to church after the fitting, but would they make it in time? Adriaan was not sure.

He has been sitting in church next to Marietjie and her family ever since they got engaged. It was his idea of spending more time together and showing everyone how serious their relationship is. Besides, he likes watching Marietjie in church, with her face being so vulnerable and gentle during the service.

At first, he tries to keep three seats open next to him: one for Marietjie, one for Jana and one for their father. That is what Marietjie does when he comes late, she keeps an empty seat for him. However, as people fill up the chairs and move closer to Adriaan, his determination weakens. After all, he is not even sure if Marietjie will make it in time. Eventually, he gives in to the requests from others to move and soon there is only one open seat next to him..

Marietjie enters the church with her sister and her father. She sees Adriaan but there is not enough space for her family to sit next to him. She would like sitting next to him, but at the same time believes that she is supposed to sit with her family, at least until the wedding. So, instead of joining Adriaan, she gives him a stern look, as if saying, "Why have you not kept three seats for us?"

He, in turn, gives her a charming smile, which conveys, "It is not my fault that you are late."

As the service begins, the Reverend's voice can be heard prominently as it echoes through the building's structure. Open your songbook at song 19 in The Book. The church congregation stood up and lifted their books, almost in unison. Jana looks at her sister. They have been rushing to get to church in time and so Marietjie is still holding Jana's letter in her hand. *How am I going to get my letter back?* thinks Jana. When everyone sits down, Marietjie, still unsure what to do with the letter, puts it into the compartment for Bibles, in front of her chair. Jana is watching her every move.

Before Jana could think of a plan, the attention is turned to Karla walking into the church wearing a short dress. It is highly unlikely that anyone in this town will come to a church meeting wearing such an attire.. The faces of a few older Tannies (aunts) show their disapproval, one of them even closes her husband's eyes as the young girl walks past. Even the Reverend is struggling to keep his eyes on The Cross.

With most of the seats occupied, Karla sees the single open one next to Adriaan and walks boldly to sit next to him. She strikes a conversation with a smile and does not seem to be bothered by the looks and the attention she is receiving. In fact, she is enjoying the moment.

Marietjie is watching the scene together with the whole congregation. She struggles to figure out who this girl is and why she is sitting next to her Adriaan. They seem to know each other and enjoy each other's company. Still struggling with her own thoughts of the situation, Marietjie hears two Tannies behind her gossiping.

"I saw this new girl walking with Adriaan this very morning. They seem to be very happy together," says one of them.

"My word! I thought Adriaan was engaged to Marietjie," says the other.

"He was engaged to Marietjie but I think they broke up. That is why they do not sit together in church anymore," says the first one.

"Poor Marietjie!" replies her friend sympathetically

.

Still in disbelief that this is happening to her, Marietjie turns around to give the Tannies a stern look reminding them that she is right there in front of them. The Tannies go quiet.

By the time Marietjie looked back, Jana had already seized the moment to grab her letter. With Marietjie being distracted, Jana manages to finally read what the note says, "Meet you at the usual spot at 11:00. Do not be late!"

The Reverend's voice has a loud tone that can be heard by all in the congregation. It is a well-rehearsed, an almost unnatural way of speaking, a form of voice art practiced by those chosen to carry The Message to the people, 'I will sing of your love and justice; to you, Lord, I will sing praise. I will be careful to lead a blameless life— when will you come to me? I will conduct the affairs of my house with a blameless heart. I will not look with approval on anything that is vile. I hate what faithless people do, I will have no part in it. The perverse of heart shall be far from me. I will have nothing to do with what is evil. Whoever slanders their neighbor in secret, I will put to silence; whoever has haughty eyes and a proud heart, I will not tolerate."

CHAPTER SIX

Heist

Away from the church, a group of young orphan boys are planning a heist. These boys are the outcasts. Their families could not or would not take care of them. The government classified them as "coloured" and by doing this, has separated them from others even further. Although many people give donations to the orphanage from time to time, they are mostly content that these kids are someone else's problem.

At "the House", as the children call it, they rise early to do the daily tasks. Daily prayer is first in the morning, followed by cleaning the old tiles and performing other chores. Initially, in 1843 the Rhenish Missionary was established as a refuge for freed slaves and was called Steinthal. Later it became the property of the Dutch Reformed Mission Church, an orphanage home to unwanted and unfortunate children.

The gates of the House remain unlocked to accommodate deliveries, but there is such a powerful sense of imprisonment that most dare not leave. Michael though, is a different story. He is a young boy with a face that has clearly been in the sun, his body with scratch marks, his clothing too big for his size. Michael is the leader of the Gang. His sense of adventure is well known - not only in the orphanage, but also outside of it. This, however, ruined his reputation in town. Parents routinely warn their children to stay away from orphan boys, whether they are part of the Gang or not.

Outside the orphanage Michael has a bad reputation, but inside the walls of the House Michael is a hero, admired by his peers and adored by younger kids. Michael and his Gang venture into the big world outside the orphanage walls, they go on treasure hunts and return to share the bounty with the rest of the kids. Most of the time they steal fruit from farms and gardens around the orphanage. Even though Michael is technically just a petty thief, he is no less than a Robin Hood to the rest of the kids.

Michael and his gang are a source of great concern for Meneer Arendse, the principal of the orphanage. He has tried both the rod and prayer to steer Michael in the right direction, but to no avail. These methods did not have the effect on Michael the way one would expect them to.

Michael takes the harsh punishment without tears, which gains him even more respect from the rest of the kids. Michael says the prayers with sincerity, yet it does not change his behaviour in the slightest way.

Meneer Arendse feels convicted that it is necessary to save the other kids from Michael's bad influence, so he is considering sending Michael away to a juvenile reformatory. The problem is, that in his heart, he, Arendse, does not believe that Michael really deserves to go there. Though he would in no way admit it publicly, he, just like everyone else in the House, likes this energetic, unruly Michael. It is as if Michael's rebellious spirit is challenging the very system, turning it inside out.

The boys of the Gang now sit down in the shade of a tree, out of sight of others, who could overhear their plans. Michael uses a stick to draw a sketch on the dusty ground to show the rest what he has in mind for their next mission.

"Here is the plan," Michael says as he continues to draw, "Hére is the house of old Tannie Wilma, the scariest old Tannie one can ever imagine…"

Sollie, the youngest of all asks in a soft voice, "Is she really a witch?"

Michael replies with a reassuring voice, "Nobody can know for sure, but you are not scared, are you?"

Braam, Michael's best friend and partner in mischief, is known for his muscle, but not for any academic ability. He is ready to tell a spooky story in a mysterious voice, "There was a boy who came to Tannie Wilma's garden late one night. It was dark and nobody could see them, so the old witch put the boy alight, just like that! and he claps his fingers to demonstrate how fast. If he did not run so fast, she would have caught him and eaten him all up."

Sollie looks at Braam, with fear written all over his young face.

"The boy ran, and ran and ran, still in flames," continues Braam. "The witch did not catch him that night, but nobody saw him again after that!... Ever!!!"

The boys all look at Braam now, the details of his story do not make sense – something does not add up. Braam, however, enjoys the frightened expression he sees on little Sollie's face.

Antonie, also known as the Brain of the Gang, shakes his head in disbelief, "I am just checking... If nòbody actually saw them, then how do yòu know what happened?"

Braam looks back at Antonie, confused that he could work that out.

In the meantime, Michael points back at the drawing on the ground, "Witch or no witch, her garden has naartjies (a type of citrus fruit), and not just any naartjies, but the sweetest you can dream of. Today we will go and get some and have a feast at the orphanage."

There is a sense of confidence on Micheals's face, enough to give the boys an injection of bravery beyond their fear of being caught, even by a witch. They are part and parcel of this adventure.

"So..., you want us to go steal the naartjies and then just run away?" Antonie asks with uncertainty.

Michael nods his head. It is a simple plan that requires them to work together quickly and efficiently.

Antonie puts his head down, having been part of many adventures with Michael, he knows that this might not end well.

Michael points back to his drawing, "To get to her yard, we have to sneak past Boet, the dog, very, very stealthily…"

Sollie once again interrupts, "Does Boet bite?" Sollie's lip quivers as he utters the words.

The rest of the gang laughs at his question.

"What?" Sollie tries to explain his concern "Some dogs only bark,…but they do not actually bite!"

Michael continues: "After passing Boet, we have to climb onto the chicken house in order to get over the gate. It is the only way - but there we might encounter a big black rooster… Stay away from him. He does not only make a lot of noise, he is also very protective of his hens, and an aggressive rooster is dangerous. If he flies up and kicks, those spurs cut like knives"

"So, is Jana coming?" Braam looks at Michael while asking.

Michael looks over to the hill, pensively. Far in the distance, the church can be seen. The other boys continue discussing the plan while Michael is zoomed out.

"So, what we really need for this mission is camouflage," pronounces Antonie.

He has read about this in an old comic book dropped off at the orphanage, the pictures showing military men from the Navy making black marks over their faces and bodies to be almost invisible at night.

Antonie shows the boys the illustration he has torn from the comic book and they start their preparation. Under the trees, the boys get old leaves and stick them to their faces and clothes with mud . This sight would be shocking for most parents. These boys are lucky, they do not need parental approval.

Next Braam starts gathering chicken feathers scattered around the sides of the gates. He starts sticking them to his body, only to realize that they make him itch. As Braam tries to get rid of the irritating feathers the other boys stick more onto his body causing a feather fight, a chase and lots of laughter.

"It is time," Michael says finally.

As they come close to Tannie Wilma's house, Michael throws a bone with enough meat on it to the dog. The dog grabs the bone and crunches it with mighty power. This buys the boys enough time to climb onto the chicken house. They try to be very quiet, but it proves to be a difficult task as the metal plates creak under their weight. The sun is baking down on the metal sheets, and the worn out shoes of the boys cannot protect their feet. It is like walking on a hot stove. The further they walk, the more they can feel the heat penetrating the soles of their shoes. It is as if the soles are melting, and more so with every step they take. Little Sollie is cringing, trying not to make any sound.

Finally, the boys are off the chicken house and over the fencing. They draw closer to the naartjie trees. Tannie Wilma's yard is filled with all kinds of plants, Christmas roses, lavender bushes, bougainvillea and more, but it is evident that the garden has seen better days. It would seem that somebody used to give a lot of care to the garden and then suddenly abandoned it.

Looking at the garden, Michael starts thinking of its owner. Michael does not believe that Tannie Wilma is a witch. *Perhaps, just an old scary-looking woman. Probably very lonely. It is very possible that no-one cares for her. She lives here all by herself, forgotten and unwanted, and gets grumpier with every passing day.*

While Michael is in thought, Braam and Antonie already help Sollie up into the tree. Sollie is a good climber and quickly makes his way up. Antonie warns Sollie, "Remember you are on the lookout. If you see the witch, you whistle as hard as you can."

Antonie and Braam start filling their pockets and plastic bags with fruit, looking up from time to time, to see if there is any movement at the windows of the house.

It is quiet....., too quiet. Antonie's bags fill up fast and he starts throwing fruit to Braam.

Sollie sees the curtain of the house move slightly. He imagines he sees the witch's eyes through the window. He is uncertain though if his imagination is playing tricks on him. It is dark in the house and Sollie looks around to see if anyone else has noticed something. He does not want to alert the rest of the Gang unnecessarily .

Braam and Antonie quickly gather some more fruit. Michael is heading towards the tree closest to the house. He cannot resist the fruit, nor the stories that might come of his bravery if he would succeed and live to tell the tale. Enthusiastically, yet carefully, Michael picks some fruit, looking back at Sollie. Sollie shows thumbs up to Michael, indicating that everything is fine.

Then suddenly Sollie sees a definite movement at the back of the house. As he clears the branch he sees an elderly lady, with unruly hair as if standing in the air. She is carrying a rifle in her hand. Sollie tries to whistle, placing his fingers together as Antonie had shown him, but no sound comes out. He tries harder, but still no success. Sollie's eyes widen as he sees that tannie Wilma is slowly approaching Michael, pointing the gun at him.

Suddenly, the chickens start cackling loudly and flying around, making everyone turn to the noise. Jana flies over the fence first, yelling. "Come now, run!"

Unsure of what is happening, Michael turns around, just to see Tannie Wilma and simultaneously hears the gun firing, hitting the soil next to him.

It feels like a slow-motion moment for the boys all figuring out what to do next.

Braam and Antonie's camouflaged bodies quickly make their way to the chicken house, towards Jana who fled to the chicken house.

Braam gives his bag to Antonie, to quickly jump over the fence onto the chicken house. Climbing over the fence, Braam falls down head first and surprises the rooster which starts pecking him. Fortunately Braam succeeds in scrambling up on the chicken house before the rooster could step back a meter or so to really start an attack on the intruder.

As Antonie tries to climb over the fence with all the bags, one of them tears on the barbed wire and the fruit falls out rolling onto the ground. Jana helps Antonie with the bags.

In the meantime Tannie Wilma is pointing the gun at Michael. Michael, still in sight of Tannie Wilma, is now at the fruit tree where Sollie is holding on, trying to hide in the branches.

"Now, Sollie! Jump!" Michael shouts.

Michael stands with his arms open, ready to catch Sollie. The young boy is scared to fall down and he closes his eyes as he jumps. They both end up falling to the ground and rolling, breaking the lavender bushes. Now is not the time to count bruises and they are up quickly, making their way towards the barbed wire past the chicken house.

Another shot is fired that ricochets off the metal plates close to Michael and Sollie. The boys duck down. When they are both over the fence, Sollie runs for his life not even seeing the growling dog. Michael looks back over the fence at the yard of old Tannie Wilma. He wants to make sure they are not being followed. He sees the old woman standing there, not furious anymore but with a look of despondency on her face. Alone and sad, Tannie Wilma slowly walks towards her broken lavender bushes. Michael sees how she struggles to move and bend down; how she tries to gently pick up the flowers and as she assesses the damage, how tears start rolling down her cheeks.

Struck, not so much by what he sees, but by what he feels on the inside, Michael recognizes a sting of pain caused by looking at the old abandoned and vulnerable woman that had just been robbed by his Gang. At that moment he would much rather have a scary witch run after him than watch this helpless old woman cry.

CHAPTER SEVEN

Feast

The Gang runs over the hills – out of sight. They are covered with dust, mud, feathers and some minor bruises. Best of all, though, they are carrying their reward. Their bravery has paid off this time.

"I thought you were on the lookout," Antonie says to Sollie, "Did you see the witch coming? Did she steal your voice?"

Sollie lowers his head.

Michael puts his hand on Sollie's shoulder and says, "It is okay, we have all been scared before."

"Scared? I was not scared. The thing is….," Sollie tries to put it into words "I cannot whistle."

Everyone looks at Sollie.

"And you only tell us now?" asks Braam.

Sollie's cheeks go red.

"Well, he is right about one thing…" Says Antonie

"About what?" asks Braam.

"Not all dogs bite!" replies Antonie. The boys laugh as they continue walking.

Michael moves closer to Jana and takes a bag from her hand, so she does not have to carry the heavy fruit.

"How did you find us?" asks Michael, "I thought that when you were late for our meeting you would not know where to find us, even if you wanted to join."

"You were talking about these fruit trees last week, so I thought you could be there," says Jana.

"Thank you, Jana," Michael says softly.

"For what?" Jana asks, surprised.

"For coming… and for saving my life" replies Michael.

"I did not save your life!" laughs Jana.

"You warned me about Tannie Wilma's presence just in time for me to escape. She could have shot me down if she came closer," explains Michael.

"Oh, no, she would not!" laughs Jana again.

"How can you be so sure? Have you not seen her aiming at me?" says Michael, upset.

"I have done a little bit of research on Tannie Wilma after you have indicated strong interest in her fruit trees" explained Jana. "When Tannie Wilma was younger, she was a huntress. She was not just doing it for fun, she excelled at it! So you see, Michael, had she been aiming at you, you would surely be dead!"

Michael tried to imagine how the woman that now struggles to even walk, used to be a huntress. *Her life must have been very different back then… How does she cope with being helpless and frail after being admired for her skills and agility?*

"I am sorry that I have not warned you about Tannie Wilma," says Jana, mistaking Michaels's quiet contemplation for resentment. "I would have come earlier if only I could. Marietjie feels she needs to control everything around her, including my every move! I get so irritated with her sometimes, I feel so trapped!" complains Jana.

"I know how it feels," agrees Michael, "At the orphanage, we have so many rules of what to do and not to do and how to do it! Plus, they call us "coloured" and say we can only be with other "coloureds". Just imagine all the places I cannot go to and the things I cannot do! You see, Jana, these rules, they work against me, against you, against all of us. That is why I choose not to follow the rules, to live my life the way I decide to, not the way someone else tells me to!"

The Gang is close to the orphanage now, so they say goodbye to Jana. Because of "the rules" they cannot afford to be seen together, "coloured" boys and a "white" girl. The Gang enters the gates of the orphanage and walks towards a small tap at the back of the House. They wash off their dirt, revealing the scrape marks they have acquired during the mission. These battle scars are their pride and joy: illustrations to the stories they will tell. The excitement starts to build up at the orphanage as the rest of the kids anticipate delicious treats and yet another story of adventurous missions. Michael, Antonie, Sollie, and Braam are handing out naartjies to the rest of the children at the orphanage.

CHAPTER EIGHT

Punishment

While the Gang and the other kids from the orphanage are enjoying their fruit feast, they hear a familiar clearing of the throat. Meneer Arendse, the principal, is standing in the shade of the house watching them. He is just standing there, not saying a word, not even moving, his hands behind his back.

Slowly, the children realise the principal is there. They try to move away from his sight and while some are quickly finishing their fruit, others try to hide them. The laughter dies out and the gloomy mood sets in as everyone understands that it is time to meet the consequences of their actions.

Meneer Arendse is a reasonable man, but in his world, right is right and wrong is wrong… All the children know what it means to sin and can recite numerous verses about being a sinner.

He knows very well that the kindness and gifts offered to them from the farmers and the community of Tulbagh are necessary for the maintenance of the orphanage. He also knows that people expect the worst of the non-white orphan kids. Even though he tries to change this perspective bit by bit, it does not come easy. It becomes an impossible mission with kids like Michael that are constantly involved in petty theft.

Meneer Arendse is sure that today's fruit feast is arranged by Michael and his Gang.

So, the time has come, he thinks to himself. *Time to set things straight and to send Michael away. This will take some paperwork and police involvement, but I need to start the process. I can no longer allow this sin to grow. Let it serve as an example for other children, so they can see that sin is punished in this House.*

He moves forward as the children move away from him and finds himself in the middle of the yard surrounded by the kids. He clears his throat once again and his deep voice resonates with fear, "God hates sin, even the smallest of sin. We should act towards others as we would act towards God."

It is clear that he is angry when he orders "Stand in a line against the wall. Hands stretched out, NOW!"

The children are hesitant but when he lifts the rod that he has been keeping behind his back, they all run towards the wall.

Sollie is in the line and his knees are shaking as Meneer Arendse comes closer. Tears are building up in Sollie's eyes.

"Turn around," he commands Sollie.

The boy trembles in fear at the voice of the principal. He slowly turns around.

Meneer Arendse pulls back his hand with the rod.

The other children look away, but not Michael.

He in fact moves quickly out of the line towards Meneer Arendse who looks at him sternly.

"It was me, Meneer," Michael says.

The other kids look at Michael with gratitude.

Sollie wants to speak up, but Antonie gestures with a shake of his head at Sollie, not to..

"You stole and carried all this fruit alone?" he asks Michael.

"Yes, Meneer," Michael responds, "I am the fastest runner, you know that."

Meneer Arendse knows that Michael is great at sports, so perhaps he could make a career of it, that is... if someone would want to invest in his training and competition participation. Of course, it is out of the question at their House, the orphanage does not have any resources for luxuries like that.

Meneer Arendse also knows that Michael has not stolen the fruit on his own, yet he is now ready to start the case against Michael and his confession will come in handy.

He nods his head and shows with his hand to the door. The others know that Michael will get a scolding to remember. Unsure if they should finish eating the fruit, the children look towards the door. Michael and the principal walk out.

It feels like time slows down, but it is mere moments before the loud sound of the rod hitting Michael can be heard. Not a sound from Michael follows the blows. Michael knows the pain of being beaten, but this pain does not in the least compare to other pains he has experienced. The pain of not being wanted, of not being good enough. Not white enough, not black enough, not loved enough. Michael knows that the red marks on his body will wash away with time, but the other scars will still hurt wherever he goes.

CHAPTER NINE

Sisters

The van Schalkwyk farmhouse is a large building with a few entrances. Jana tries to enter the house quietly, her dress smudged in mud from the mission with the orphan boys.

It is difficult not to make any noise with the creaky old wooden floors. As she walks past the living room she sees their dog Daantjie sleeping on the floor. Trying not to wake him, she tiptoes through the living room filled with wedding décor, glasses, plates, gifts, flower pots and more. Jana walks carefully to avoid leaving any marks on the wedding inventory.

Daantjie wakes up and looks at Jana.

Jana covers her lips with one finger, asking Daantjie to be quiet.

Daantjie turns his head to the side, trying to figure out what Jana's gesture means.

As she walks quietly, Jana hears voices, coming from Marietjie's bedroom. They become louder and more aggressive, so Jana can hear the whole conversation.

"Marietjie, I understand that you are stressed… But, honestly? To be jealous of this? I think it is really stupid," says Adriaan

"Stupid? Do you know that the town Tannies say we have broken up because of this new girl? Why do I know nothing about her?" asks Marietjie.

"Well, maybe you know nothing about her because you just do not care," replies Adriaan.

"What is that supposed to mean?" Marietjie says angry.

"It means that I am not on your priority list! You are too busy to even care where I am or what I am doing," Adriaan retorts

.

"So, now it is all my fault! You have a great reason to spend time with another girl just because I am too busy arranging our wedding? After a pause Marietjie asks, "Tell me the truth, do you like her?"

"Marietjie, I do not like her. The problem is that I… I am not sure I like you right now. The closer it gets to the wedding the less time we spend together, the more we fight. There is just not enough space for me in your busy schedule!" Adriaan responds.

"If you do not like me... then... just leave!" Marietjie exclaims.

"Marietjie, I am trying to explain..." Adriaan continues.

"You have to leave right now," pronouncing these last words Marietjie is almost screaming.

Jana has never heard Marietjie scream. In fact, it was always her, Jana, throwing the tantrums. *It must be really serious*, Jana thinks, frightened by her sister's explosion.

In a second Jana sees Adriaan running out of the house.

She walks to Marietjie's room and sees her sister through the open door. She can also see the pain so clearly as if it is another object in the room, just like a bed or a lampshade.

Marietjie is looking at the photo of her mother and father on their wedding day. This is the photo Marietjie keeps on her bedside table.

She walks into the room and closer to Marietjie but Marietjie seems to be far away and does not look up at Jana.

She notices the photo Marietjie is holding, a sweet yet painful memory.

"Our mother was really beautiful," Jana says looking at the photo.

Marietjie gets up hearing her voice and puts the photo back onto the bedside table. She still tries to avoid eye contact with Jana.

Jana wonders what Marietjie is thinking at that moment. She could never completely understand her sister, partially because she has never expressed her emotions strongly. Unlike Jana, she has always seemed to be cool, calm and collected. She did not scream or cry, not even when their mother died.

That was until today…when Marietjie screamed at Adriaan.

Poor Marietjie, thinks Jana. *Whatever that is, Marietjie must be at breaking point!*

To cheer her sister up, Jana says, "I think you will be just as beautiful as our mother on your wedding day."

"I do not know if the wedding is going to happen," Marietjie's voice is soft, filled with uncertainty and sadness.

Jana jumps onto the bed and invites Marietjie with a gesture to come and sit on the bed next to her.

Marietjie sits on the edge of the bed and folds her arms on her knees, then she starts speaking, "I feel everything around me is falling apart and I feel it is my fault. I am so sad and angry at the same time. How can that be before my wedding?"

"I also feel angry, Marietjie," responds Jana. "I am angry at everything and everyone… and very often at you."

Marietjie and Jana look at each other.

Jana continues, "I really miss our mother. And father, well, he is never really here."

"He works… It's not easy for him either," Marietjie replies with sadness.

"But he works all the time!" says Jana.

"He loves us and he loves our mother. Love can be complicated," explains Marietjie.

"Do you remember how we would come and snuggle in bed with mom?" asks Jana.

Marietjie smiles as she recalls a fond memory, "And your feet were always ice cold because you refused to wear shoes".

"And you were always upset when my cold feet touched yours," responds Jana.

They look at each other again.

Then the smile leaves Marietjie's face and she says, "It was really special. We did not even realize how happy we were back then."

"It felt like happiness was normal, that it would last forever," continues Jana.

"To know it can never be like that again, kills me," says Marietjie. "We can never be like that again!"

"You are wrong, Marietjie. We can. Come here, closer to me, please," Jana says.

Marietjie climbs higher onto the bed, following Jana. They lie down close to each other.

"Marietjie, listen to me! Close your eyes. Remember her voice, her eyes. The sunny days together outside, the cold nights in front of the fireplace. Remember how we were here together in this bed and how it felt. No one can take these memories away from us."

Marietjie remembers the touch of the mother's hand, the warmth of the fireplace that was burning in the living room, their father's happy face in the mornings before he left to go to the farmlands. Marietjie and Jana lie together with their eyes closed and their hands touching.

CHAPTER TEN

Dinner

The smell of warm pumpkin fritters and baked meat is pleasant to Karla, who is sitting at the big, ball and claw wooden table in the dining room with Tannie Truia, Oom Ben and their only son Hanri. The house with its paintings, photographs, vintage vases, and books is an illustration of the family's farming history in the valley of Tulbagh.

While Ben Coetzee remained on the family farm, as a custom for the eldest son in Afrikaans families, Karla's father moved to the Netherlands where he studied plant growth in greenhouses and with time achieved certain success.

Ben had no interest in visiting his brother in the Netherlands. His world was here, in Tulbagh, on the farm, close to his fields and animals, where his great grandfather planted big oak trees to mark the road to the entrance of their estate. For Ben, the land was a testimony to the pioneers of South Africa who came and made it their home, who turned the earth and grew the first crops where nothing else had been planted before.

Truia walks into the dining room with a plate of warm pumpkin fritters.

"You probably cannot remember all about the town anymore," starts Truia. "It is quite a special place. Hanri can show you around." Truia looks at Hanri at this suggestion she makes.

"I am sure she does not need a tour guide for our little town," Hanri responds.

"Hanri, do not be difficult. Show this young lady the town, please. Of course, if you do not mind being taken around by such a grump, Karla," Truia says with a smile.

"I do not mind," Karla smiles back.

"She has already walked down the main street and she has visited the church. To be honest, that is all there is to see," Hanri says.

Ben is irritated with Hanri's lack of respect for the town of Tulbagh and responds with a stern voice, "That is quite enough, Hanri! I do not want to hear your negative ideas of our town. You, young people, grow up with so many privileges and still, you throw them away."

It is quiet at the table, uncomfortable, with only the sound of Ben's fork on his plate as he takes another bite.

Hanri breaks the silence after it has become almost unbearable, "My father believes I have to farm because his father and his father's father farmed on this land and in this town."

Ben hits his large fist on the table, swallowing his food before he starts speaking, "I will not tolerate such disrespect. You are still under my roof."

Truia would love to salvage this awkward moment but does not know what to say, she loves both her husband and her son and she feels very embarrassed that Karla sees them fight.

The table becomes quiet again.

"May I go to my room? I still feel very tired after the long flight," Karla excuses herself from this uncomfortable setting.

PART TWO

CHAPTER ONE

Tulbagh

It is an early Monday morning on 29th September, 1969 in the town of Tulbagh and Karla and Hanri walk down the street together. Children are making their way to school dressed in their uniforms and shops are opening their doors for another day of business

At the Post Office people are waiting outside. There are two windows where the public is served – one for white people and the other for non-whites. People line up in their groups waiting for their turn to be served. Karla can hear the friendly laughter of two domestic workers. One of them came to collect the post for her boss, the other, to send money to her relatives.

To Karla the whole scene is strange. Since she left so long ago, she does not remember much of Apartheid, but now she can see the world of segregation clearly and remembers her parents' words about it being dangerous to separate people against their will.

White people live in green neighbourhoods with paved roads, sidewalks and gardens. They stay in lush homes that often have swimming pools and even tennis courts. The black and coloured people who are employed there and stay in these rich suburbs have to get special permission to live in "Boy's quarters" or "Worker homes". These employees are often quite far from their own families and do not see them on a daily basis and they know the rules and times when they have to be home and stay out of the streets in these white suburbs..

On the farms, families are fortunate enough to stay together in little farm holding homes. They still have to carry the hated passbooks, which reflects that they have approval to stay there.

Apartheid is not taught here, but it becomes part of you, no matter on which side of the colour spectrum you are. It is an embedded, unconscious, almost automatic colour sorting world.

Hanri and Karla go past the petrol station and Karla overhears a woman next to her car talking to the petrol attendant. She has paid for the petrol and now asks if her small daughter may use the toilet. The little girl is clearly in a desperate need, but the toilet is marked *"For whites only"*. The attendant shakes his head at this question and walks away. Karla is a bit rattled by what she has just witnessed. She looks around to see how other people will react, but no-one seems to care. Even Hanri does not appear to be bothered by this at all. As they walk past, Karla can see the little girl's sad frightened face.

The cousins continue walking through the town. Karla notices a white baby that is bottle-fed by her African nanny. She is sitting on a bench marked for nannies. They walk past the butcher shop and an advert on the window states, "Servants and boys meat only 80 cents" catches her eye.

Back in the Netherlands, Karla also saw a large influx of immigrants from Dutch colonies. She heard many different accents and most people also settled within their own community and language group. The immigrants often obtained low level jobs and faced great difficulty with the language and culture, but over time many of those immigrants were integrated into the Dutch society just like any other citizen.

"About yesterday," Hanri says to Karla. "I am sorry you had to be in the middle of the family drama."

"It does not bother me, Hanri. What is it all about?" They continue walking down the road.

Hanri shakes his head, "The thing is, being the only son, the responsibility of continuing farming is mine. Every time I look at my father I can feel that responsibility. The problem is, I really do not want to become a farmer. I care about my parents and the farm but my heart is not in farming."

"You cannot change who you are, can you?" asks Karla.

"Maybe I can. Maybe I should at least try, but all I want to do is run away from this burden," says Hanri cheerlessly.

"It is better to change direction halfway than to be wrong all the way. I think you should follow your true calling. What is your true calling, Hanri?" asks Karla.

"To be honest, I do not know yet, but if I get stuck in this little town I am afraid I will never figure it out, Karla," he replies

"I guess you will not then," she says.

Hanri keeps quiet, thinking about what had just been said.

As they walk further, Karla sees Adriaan.

"Do you know this young man?" she asks, deciding to do some research on the young man that has caught her attention.

"I do", replies Hanri. "In this small town everyone knows everything about everyone. This is Adriaan, a good friend of mine. He is getting married some time soon and I am invited."

Karla is quiet for a moment. Trying not to show her disappointment at the news, she asks, "Is he engaged to Marietjie van Schalkwyk?"

"Yes, you are right! How do you know him?" Hanri asks.

"Because I have an invitation to their wedding too, but it is unlikely that I will be attending," Karla replies in a somewhat strange tone of voice.

Hanri senses the change of mood in Karla, but is unable to figure out what has just happened. They walk in silence for a few more minutes. After that Karla, still in a bad mood, asks him to take her home. While they drive home, no word is exchanged and Hanri is thinking of the prospect of staying in the Tulbagh for the rest of his life. When they arrive home, he feels absolutely convicted that he has to run away from this place. He immediately starts packing his most important belongings, his documents and his savings. He has made up his mind - before dark he will jump into his car and drive off into the dark, leaving a short letter in his room.

CHAPTER TWO

Rats

The next morning after the sisters have fallen asleep together in Marietjie's big bed, Jana opens her eyes and somehow feels strange. She does not know what it is: is it her seeing a different room upon awakening, or is it the fact that nobody is demanding that she wakes up. Jana feels good and full of energy.

Today is going to be a great day, thinks Jana. Marietjie is still asleep and Jana leaves the room quietly. She rushes to her own bedroom and gets dressed for school as quickly as she can. She plaits her hair, holding the hair strings with her teeth, since both her hands are busy. Only after she is done, she finally takes a glance at the clock to see if she has time to grab some breakfast before leaving for school.

She is so used to getting everything done hurriedly in the last few minutes that she is very surprised to see it is actually early, not late. Staring at the clock for a moment, not believing what she sees, she gets even more excited about the day to come. Jana runs downstairs and into the kitchen.

"More, Grace!" Jana exclaims.

Grace looks at Jana in disbelief.

"Why did you wake up so early today?" asks Grace, continuing with the breakfast preparation.

"I have no idea!" replies Jana, shining with joy.

"Is Marietjie still in her bedroom?" asks Grace, concerned.

"She is still sleeping" replies Jana triumphantly. "Maybe I should wake hér up?" she chuckles.

"Do you think she is all right?" Grace is not sure what to make of such a dramatic change in the morning routine.

"I think she is," Jana reassures Grace. "And since Marietjie is asleep, I will today do whatever Marietjie does in the morning to help you."

"In the morning Marietjie is busy waking you up!" laughs Grace. "But if you want to help, go outside and help Sune hang up the clothes. When I am done with breakfast I will call you."

Jana and little Sune are hanging up the clothes. Sune goes to pick up another garment when she sees a rat running next to the basket with wet clothes. She shrieks and hides behind Jana, frightened. Jana looks down and sees the rat. Instinctively Jana stomps her foot towards the rat to chase it away. It immediately runs into the bushes, but Sune is still hiding behind Jana.

"Just a stupid old rat, nothing to be scared of," Jana reassures Sune, who is still clinging onto Jana.

She lets go of Jana, but as soon as she moves back to the basket, she sees another rat running past, then two more. This time Sune screams, and runs back into the house. Jana takes the basket and follows Sune.

"Rats...Rats!!!" Sune is overwhelmed. "There are rats everywhere!"

"There is always a rat or two around the farm, Sune", explains Grace while setting the table.

"No, Grace, I have never seen so many rats running around here like this!" exclaims Jana.

Knowing that Jana is not easily scared, Grace stops working.

"Famines, pestilence and fearful sights and signs shall be from heaven," says Sune solemnly. Both Grace and Jana look at Sune in surprise.

"Pastor spoke of this, The End of Times," Sune almost whispers.

Grace leaves the kitchen to go outside. She looks around from the stoep (porch) of the house from where she can see far. The valley seems peaceful though. The farm workers are walking in the distance and nothing seems out of the ordinary.

She returns to the girls, "I have not seen any rats now, but they might have a nest somewhere close by. I will tell Meneer, when he returns. He will be home late tonight as he has some important meetings regarding wine export in Cape town." She then finishes setting the table while the girls are helping her quietly.

CHAPTER

THREE

Snakes

Michael, Sollie, Antonie and Braam are outside in the yard next to the House. Michael and Braam are digging with large spades, while the other two boys are clearing the grass and weeds. This is a new project of Principal Arendse - he is starting a vegetable garden to supplement the poor ration of the kids. As a way of punishment, the Gang members are obliged to do the hardest work of turning the soil, while the others have a recreational break after lunch. The soil is mostly rock and clay. *Not ideal for a vegetable garden but one needs to utilise what you have been given*, Micheal thinks to himself.

As they are busy working and sweating in the hot afternoon sun, the boys notice a snake slither past.

"A Rattlesnake!" Antonie alerts the others.

As the boys watch the rattlesnake coming closer and closer, they notice another snake at a distance.

Michael takes a swift step towards the rattlesnake and cuts off its head with one blow from the spade.

"We need to get rid of it, otherwise more snakes might come for revenge if we leave the dead snake here," suggests Braam.

"Let us show it to the other kids first before we do it!" suggests Michael.

"Be careful of the head," warns Antonie. "It is still poisonous and it can still bite!"

"How can a dead snake bite?" wonders Braam.

"It is not dead yet. Snakes are coldblooded and have slower metabolism, so they die slower too," explains Antonie.

Braam turns the dead snake's body with his spade and as he does it the snake wriggles on the spot.

"All right," says Michael. "Let us then get rid of the head, so it does not bite anyone."

With these words Michael picks up the snake's head with his spade and throws it away.

When the head lands in the bushes close by, they hear the rustling noise and yet another snake slithers out and then back into the bushes.

"It must be the witch!" exclaims Sollie. "She has sent the snakes for us!"

"You are right, Sollie! I have never seen so many snakes in one day," confirms Braam.

"An increased number of snakes might be telling us of some weather change, like a storm that is coming," announces Antonie.

"How can snakes predict the weather?" asks Braam.

"There is some science behind this. I have read it in a book," Antonie replies. "When storms are coming, the pressure at the surface of the earth drops. The birds are believed to sense the change in the air pressure, that is how the people can predict certain types of weather. It is said that birds fly low when storms are coming."

"I have heard that cows can predict storms when they all lie down together. The sheep do the same," confirms Sollie, relieved that there might be another simple explanation for the snake's invasion.

"Bees, butterflies and ladybugs disappear before the storm and ants build bigger hills to protect their underground homes," adds Antonie.

"I doubt there will be a storm soon, the day is so bright and sunny. Have you read anything specific about snakes?" Michael asks .

"Not really, but I believe that animals' strange behaviour can indicate something that they feel and we do not."

"If it is true, we should finish this digging before it starts pouring," Michael urges his friends and they continue working.

CHAPTER FOUR

First Shakes

The sun has set about three hours earlier and darkness has long filled the valley. Workers are at their homes, clearing the table after dinner, washing dishes, preparing for a new day. Some are getting ready for bed and many kids are already sleeping. Some lights in the valley go on while others go off.

At this time Grace and Sune are home too. Jana is asleep. She was tired because she was up early that morning and Marietjie had sent her to bed. Father has not yet returned from his trip to Cape Town.

Marietjie is standing all alone in the living room filled with the details of her wedding preparation: cards, vases, candles... She thinks of the wedding itself and what amount of work she has done to put this event together and make it special. *What does this wedding mean to me anyway?* She wonders.

Not so much if compared to the lifetime with the person I love. I am expected to have a big wedding, and so I do my best to organise this celebration. This is understandable. What does not make sense though, is how I allowed the most important thing to slip in the process. How did I let our relationship break?

Her thoughts are interrupted by the clock, striking 10 o'clock. Daantjie, their dog, starts barking.

"Daantjie… shh," Marietjie tries to hush the dog. "It is just a clock".

Daantjie keeps on barking.

"Daantjie, please! Jana is resting," Marietjie is getting annoyed.

The dog stops barking for a few seconds and then it starts howling.

"Why does no-one ever listen to me?" Marietjie exclaims. "If you do not stop barking I will chase you out of the house!" Marietjie says pointing at the door.

As if understanding, Daantjie stops making noise and hides under the table.

"That is much better!" Marietjie is pleased that her threat has worked .

At that same moment Marietjie starts feeling a strange tremor under her feet and hears an extremely loud rumbling sound. Terrified, she sees the walls vibrating, and the wedding décor on the table moving around. It is as if one is inside a tumbler dryer with no sense of up or down. She tries to reach out to the closest wall but struggles to find her steps. Within moments dust fills the air, and the power suddenly goes off, leaving her in the pitch dark.

The next moment she hears Jana screaming. The sound of Jana screaming alarms Marietjie. She tries to find her balance and takes a few steps towards Jana's bedroom, but falls down. The shaking continues. After a few seconds that felt incredibly long to Marietjie, the shaking stops. She tries to rush between broken furniture and décor through the dark living room. The sound of broken glass underneath her feet does not bother Marietjie. Daantjie is howling somewhere in the corner out of sight.

As Marietjie approaches Jana's bedroom door, she sees that a big wooden support bar fell down in the corridor, hitting the doorpost to Jana's bedroom. This resulted in the door being squeezed tight into the frame. Inside, Jana is terrified of what had just happened. Marietjie pushes the door trying to budge it open, but it only moves a centimeter or two.

"Jana, Jana.. are you there? Are you all right?" Marietjie asks with panic in her voice.

"Marietjie?" Jana replies softly. " I cannot see anything. Even the window is gone… The wall fell in. What has just happened?"

"I do not know but I need to get you out of there," Marietjie responds, possibilities racing through her mind as to how she would manage to do it. She pushes the wooden support with all her might. The large beam is way too heavy for her to move. She pushes again, trying to budge the door, but to no avail. Marietjie turns around trying to use her legs to push against the door with her weight.

She can hear Jana's frightened voice, "I am so scared. If it happens again, I think the roof will fall down on me."

"I will get you out Jana! I will!" Marietjie tries to push the beam harder, her hand scuffing against the rough wood, but the beam does not budge an inch. In despair Marietjie starts hitting the beam, hurting herself.

CHAPTER FIVE

The End Of The World

B en and Truia go to bed early. They are fast asleep when the earthquake starts. The shaking and the loud noise are such a shock to Truia's body that she starts screaming, even before she is completely awake.

"Stop screaming, woman, and start praying. It is the end of the world," says Ben. "The Bible says that The Lord Almighty will come with thunder and earthquake and great noise, with windstorm and tempest and flames of a devouring fire."

After some minutes the tremors have stopped, but Truia can still hear the shouting, crying and screaming of petrified farmworkers and their children.

"Look!" Ben points at the window, where a bright light can be seen in the distance, a fire flaring up on the mountain.

Ben and Truia can see it spread rapidly. They sit together in bed and watch the mountains in the dark, light up with bright red stripes of fire. It is a majestic spectacle.

As if tremors and fires have not been enough, water starts dripping through the ceiling. After a strange creaking, tearing sound, a part of the roof falls onto the lower end of the bed. Together with the roof, the water pours down. It all happens so close to Ben and Truia that they have to pull back frightened...

"Wait, wait... The Bible says that the human race will not be destroyed with water again," says Ben contemplating. "It is not our time, Truia!"

Ben takes Truia's hand firmly and leads her out of the room.

In the corridor Ben calls, "Hanri, Karla! Get out of your rooms!"

Karla's door opens and she comes out slowly, visibly in a state of shock. The house has been turned into chaos in mere seconds.

"Hanri, get out now!," Ben says in a stern voice.

"Ben," Truia says softly and with sadness. "Hanri has left".

"What is he doing out so late?" Ben asks angrily.

"I mean, he has left Tulbagh. He has left for good," replies Truia.

Ben turns quiet.

"I saw him leave after dinner. I told him he should say goodbye to you, but he did not want to," the last words Truia utters so softly, she almost whispers.

Ben seems to be outraged, "Coward!"

"We need to get out of here, before the house falls down," says Karla. Together they feel their way outside through the long dark corridor.

Ben pushes hard to get the front door open. Outside the air is still quivering with echoes of the loud noise that has taken over the once peaceful valley. Ben can see farm workers in the distance, they are also leaving their houses in a rush. There is a father carrying a little girl out of the house, she is coughing from the dust. It is difficult to see if anyone is hurt.

Ben's foreman runs towards him, "Meneer, the water is streaming down the farm road. I think the pipes have burst open. We have to close the pipes, or we will not have any water to farm with. Summer is on the way."

Ben agrees, "You go and make sure the workers all stay out of their houses. See if anyone is hurt. The mountains are on fire. If it comes closer, take the truck and start driving people away to safety. Women and kids first."

"Ja, Meneer," The foreman nods his head. "What about the pipes?"

Ben looks up the road, "I will take care of it myself", he says with determination in his voice. "I have to do it myself. I need you here to take care of the people."

It is not far to drive with a bakkie, but the road is extremely difficult with cracks and loose rocks scattered all over. As Ben gets closer to the broken pipes, the road gets slippery and muddy with water. He has to park some distance away and walk further to the site where water is bursting from under the ground.

CHAPTER SIX

Church Street

Karla is outside. Truia talks to the foreman, who is loading people on the back of the bakkie. Truia looks up to the fire in the mountain, knowing she has to wait for Ben and if Hanri by any chance would return. Truia holds Karla's hand tight and helps her up to the back of the bakkie. Karla's ears are still ringing from the loud sound of the trembles and the emotional shock of what is unfolding. The foreman drives towards town. The road is filled with cracks and bumps and they drive slowly to avoid getting stuck. The loud crying and hysteria of people can be heard as they get closer to town. The foreman stops. A young farm worker with a little child is close to the road. The child is badly injured and quickly they move to assist the child, to take her to hospital. Karla climbs off the bakkie to make space for the child and mother. She walks down the street in disbelief. It feels surreal that the street that was still peaceful this morning now lies in ruin.

Through what appears to be a cloud of smoke and dust, Karla finds her way to Church street. This uniquely South African place, renowned for its buildings in Cape Dutch, Victorian and Edwardian styles, dating back to the early 1800.s is almost unrecognizable now. Windows are broken, roofs have fallen in. Some walls have large cracks, others are not there anymore. Karla can see naked bricks of the previously plastered walls. She notices shifted, cracked and misplaced columns. Karla can see right into the abandoned houses because many walls have shifted away from each other.

People are outside, many of them are wearing pyjamas and night clothes. They are scared. Some are praying, some are taking their precious possessions out.. Some people are crying, others moaning,. The dogs are frightened too and whining

.

The police arrive at the scene of the earthquake. The officer announces, "You CANNOT go home under any circumstances." People still go in and out. They fetch blankets, mattresses, some even take out beds. A lot of people make fires. There are those who try to sleep again.

This incredible scene is lit by the burning mountains. The shaking caused rocks to collide with a force that resulted in sparks, which have started fires.

Karla is walking down Church street when she feels another tremor hitting the town. It is an aftershock - typical for earthquakes. It feels like the road is rolling towards Karla.

What was solid ground a few seconds ago is now lifting up and down in waves.

The roaring rumbling resembles the sound of thunder and people start screaming in fear. Those who happened to be inside are rushing outside and squeezing through whatever is left of the doors.

One of the electrical poles falls over, pulling at and tearing the electrical wires. The sparks fly everywhere. Karla stops immediately and instinctively covers her head from the sparks. The road keeps on rolling and wobbling for the duration of the tremor.

After the tremor stopped, Karla follows a familiar road to the church, a road which is now marked with cracks. She feels extremely lonely, watching families clinging together, and at this very moment she realises with acute clarity that she does not belong here. Her place is not in Tulbagh. She has become Dutch, she just had not noticed when it happened.

She follows a broad crack that is leading right to the steps of the church and stops there. There are large stones everywhere around the church, but the building itself appears to be intact. Right there at the steps covered with dust, Karla is praying. She asks God for mercy to survive this disaster and to return back home to her parents. Karla's prayer has never been more sincere.

CHAPTER SEVEN

Pipes

Minutes before the earthquake, Hanri is driving on the mountain side, away from the valley, away from Tulbagh. His is the only car on the road at that time. He is driving slowly as the road is not lit up. He orientates himself with his car lights and retro reflective cat's eyes on the road. The radio is playing a happy tune.

Suddenly the car starts swerving, as if from a flat tire. A strange sound follows and Hanri, unsure of what to make of it, slows down. The wheels start bouncing and Hanri struggles to keep control of the car. He wants to check the tyres and stops, but before he can exit, the road lifts up and hits the car.

He has never seen anything like that. With nowhere to go, he holds onto the steering wheel while tremors continue.

On the one side of his car is the mountain, on the other is a deep valley. Both could be fatal upon impact.

Small rocks start rolling down the mountain, some of them landing on the car roof, which is instantly covered in dust.

As suddenly as it has started, the earthquake stops. All becomes quiet after the loud roar of the tremors. He climbs out to examine his car. It is severely damaged on the outside.

Feeling safe for the moment, He turns to the valley to watch Tulbagh in the distance. In the dark he cannot make out what is going on in town. Instead he sees flames flaring up on the mountain, quickly turning into dangerous bushfires.

Hanri makes a u-turn and drives back as quickly as the road, covered with cracks and stones, allows. He drives to his house and sees his mother outside, quietly crying. She is not hurt, she says, father and Karla are fine too, but Truia has been very worried about Hanri driving on the dangerous mountain pass. Truia's tears of joy upon seeing Hanri now mix with those caused by the tragedy of the earthquake. She tells him that his father went to fix the pipes all by himself and he drives off to go and help his father.

On the hillside Ben is trying to close the pump, his arms covered in thick mud. His efforts seem futile. With a loud noise and bright light Hanri's car approaches, but Ben does not look in that direction. Ben is focused on what he is doing, and feels he is failing to finish the job by himself.

Hanri sees his father covered in dirt and mud, standing in the murky water, struggling. He is not sure why, maybe because of the strange lighting of the car lights, but he cannot recognise the strong stubborn man he knows his father to be. At this moment he sees a much older, almost desperate person that has been left alone to deal with something beyond his capacity. It hurts him to see his father like that. *I did not not mean to leave you all alone. I did not not realise you needed me that much*, Hanri thinks to himself and without saying a word joins his father.

Ben, drenched in mud, is trying to get to the valve to stop the flow. Water is gushing out and flowing over the hill. The pipes are old, and need to be replaced, but for now all they need to do is to close the waterflow altogether. Ben has located the shut-off valve, but it appears to be stuck. Together, Hanri and his father try to turn the valve that closes the waterflow, but it is difficult with their hands being wet and muddy. Hanri finally puts his arms around the bottom in a firm grip while his father takes the top. Finally they manage to pull the valve to the other side and the waterflow becomes less and less until it stops completely.

They climb out of the muddy puddle created by the burst pipes. Ben sits down on the grass, exhausted. He tries to clear some mud off his face. Hanri sits down next to his father. For a moment Ben sees his little boy again, sitting on this hill with him, looking over the valley. So many moments they have shared on this piece of land and so many fights they have fought because of it.

The cold mist of the valley starts setting in. Father and son sit in silence; do not look at each other, both unsure what to say.

"Thank you for your help," Ben breaks the silence. "To be honest, I did not think you would ever return to Tulbagh."

"I am sorry I did not say goodbye before leaving," says Hanri.

"When I was young," Ben continued after a pause. "There was only one road for me, farming. I have never doubted it, I accepted it. I have never searched for other opportunities or a world bigger than this town. I have always thought you are arrogant and cannot see what you have been given. I thought you wanted to hurt your mother and me on purpose, but then you came back. Despite all the fighting you showed me you are not the lazy coward I feared you were and that you actually do care about your mother and myself and did not intend to hurt us."

"I have also learned something," Hanri says. "Tonight I have learned that you need me here. I just never realised how much. Maybe you are right. Maybe I need to stay here. Maybe I was a coward."

It is silent between them for a moment as they both stare over the valley.

Taking a deep breath Ben responds, "You have always loved learning, reading books, and were interested in the world outside this town. Go and study, follow your heart and if you do come back to this farm, it should be because you want to, not because you have to. Your mom and I will be here, whether you come to visit, or whether you come home to stay. We will be right here"

CHAPTER EIGHT

Sugar And Candles

At the time the earthquake starts, the children of the orphanage are already in bed. Those who are sleeping, wake up feeling a strange vibration and a rumbling sound that grows louder and louder, like an approaching train on a silent night. It takes only seconds before the old House starts to tumble. The children try to reach out to each other, their terrified screams are overwhelmed by the loud sound of the rumbling and the crashing of objects falling and shaking around. The sound grows more intense, deafening: the crashing dishes that the children have packed away neatly, falling pots, rattling roof and bookcases being overturned by an incredible impact of the earthquake. It sounds as if the building itself is groaning in pain, with glass shattering and plaster falling off the walls. The power goes off and the children are left in the darkness - terrified.

Meneer Arendse enters the dark space when the first tremor is over. He lives right here in the orphanage house, unlike other teachers who come for the day and leave in the evening.

His harsh voice that often frightens the children, now brings a sense of reassurance, "We need to leave the House."

Many of the kids do not understand what had just happened as none of them has ever experienced an earthquake. They are looking at each other in disbelief, they have never left the House at night before.

Meneer Arendse sees their confusion and understands that the children deserve an explanation, "What has just happened can happen again, so we need to go outside. We will be safer there. Do you understand?"

"Ja, Meneer," say some children, others nod their heads, some are just looking at Meneer Arendse with eyes full of fear – though he cannot see their expressions in the dark.

"Take each others' hands and make sure everyone goes outside. Now, follow me," Meneer Arendse says with a sense of urgency.

The kids make a little chain, holding hands as they slowly follow Meneer Arendse through the dark room. Some overturned bunker beds lie against each other and block their way, they have to step over wooden planks, broken glass and some other objects which they cannot see properly in the dark. The children gather outside, some have bruises, but most are just sad and scared .

Meneer Arendse does not know how long they will stay outside, so he decides to fetch candles, but he does not want to leave the frightened kids alone. The principal knows two agile boys, perfect for this task.

"Michael, Antonie, we need candles and matches… you know where they are kept," says the principal.

Michael consents and Meneer Arendse gives the keys to the outside shed to Michael. Normally, the children are not allowed to touch these keys, but tonight everything seems to be out of the ordinary. It is as if the whole world has been turned upside down, the whole order of things.

Michael and Antonie start walking to the shed.

"And sugar…Bring a big bag of sugar," adds Meneer Arendse.

Outside the building is a cool room, where the supplies are being stored. It is more or less intact after the earthquake, but the darkness inside makes it difficult to find anything, as in here things have also fallen from shelves during the tremor . Michael and Antonie have to feel around to get an idea of where what is. The sound of matchboxes falling down when they touched them, got them their first necessary object. With a lit up match they quickly discover the box filled with candles. Michael lights up a candle and their quest continues.

"Sugar, sugar, sugar," Michael keeps saying to himself looking around the mess of all the broken bottles and holders. In the corner the boys see a big bag of sugar.

Michael and Antonie nod their heads. Antonie starts pulling and pushing the bag of sugar cubes towards the door. Michaels has to blow his candle out to help him. Then they take out the box with candles and matches.

Outside the children are standing close to each other, some still holding hands. Meneer Arendse orders them to stand in a line so he could count them to make sure they were all there. On the first count someone is missing. Meneer Arendse counts again with the same result.

"Look at your friends. Who is not here?" asks the principal.

"It must be Michael and Antonie, Meneer. They went to fetch candles," says Braam.

"I know about them," responds Meneer Arendse with irritation. "Someone else is missing".

Kids look at each other.

"Meneer Arendse, where is Sollie? I do not see him anywhere." Braam says with concern. The kids look around, trying to locate Sollie. Meneer Arendse is afraid that Sollie might still be in the House. If that is true, he needs to be evacuated as soon as possible. It is dangerous inside and this is not a task that the principal can give to anyone else. Meneer Arendse has to do it himself.

Meneer Arendse holds Braam around the shoulders looking him straight in the eye. "Braam you make sure they all stay here. I will go back inside to search for Sollie,"

Braam understands how serious this task is, and as much as he wants to go search for Sollie, he has to obey.

Meneer Arendse enters the House. The building itself creaks, as some stones are out of place. It is not safe to enter, as the old building can fall at any moment, should there be another tremor, but Sollie might be in there and Meneer Arendse has no choice but to go look for him.

The moonlight brings mere drops of light through the open cracks of the building and shattered glass windows.

"Sollie! Sollie!" calls the principal.

The cold hard floor hits Meneer Arendse as he falls down tripping over some object which he cannot see clearly. He cuts his hand on a piece of shattered glass.

Meneer Arendse calls out again, "Sollie! Sollie!"

No one answers.

The principal stops and listens carefully. He hears some noise in the corner of the long bedroom where Sollie sleeps with some of the other boys. The murmuring sound gets louder and louder as he slowly approaches. Three bunker beds are lying against each other, holding up a piece of the ceiling that has fallen down. There, under the bunker beds he locates Sollie.

Meneer Arendse is relieved to find Sollie and the principal stretches his hands to Sollie, but one of the beds moves by accident. The pillar of this bed tilts and shifts the bed, a piece of ceiling falls and breaks next to Sollie. The little boy shrieks.

"Sollie, we need to go now. Please, give me your hands," Meneer Arendse is trying to convince Sollie to trust him and oblige.

"The witch. She is real… She is angry because we stole her fruit," whispers Sollie.

Knowing the next tremor of an after-shock might bring the roof down and the beds might not keep up the weight much longer, Mr Arendse is trying to reach out to get Sollie, but the boy is too deep under the beds.

"Come on, Sollie…" says the principal as he manages to get hold of Sollie's leg, but the little boy holds onto the pole of the bed, refusing to let go, screaming in fear. Meneer Arendse feels the poles of the beds move as he tries to pull Sollie out, so he lets go of Sollie's leg. Sollie crawls deeper under the bed.

Meneer Arendse looks up in despair and sees a cross hanging skew on the wall, lit by moonlight coming through the broken roof.

"Lord, show me the way," he prays softly.

After the prayer Meneer Arendse tries to lure Sollie out, "You can sit here all alone, or you can be really brave and come with me. Then you will get a sugar cube."

The room is quiet as the principal is waiting for an answer.

A little voice from under the bed utters, "Two cubes?"

"Three cubes!" exclaims Meneer Arendse with new hope. He bends down to stretch under the bed. He gives Sollie both hands, one of them is still bleeding from the glass cut. Sollie grabs his hands and Meneer Arendse can finally pull Sollie out. Together they move out of the damaged House as fast as they can.

Outside the orphanage Micheal and Antonie have already started lighting candles. They hand a candle to each child and the scene resembles a primitive nativity play.

CHAPTER NINE

Door

In the dark corridor Marietjie hits the wooden beam that has damaged the doorpost and makes access to her sister's room impossible. She is hitting it with a fury she has never experienced before. All the internal frustration with her present situation she now puts into the fight with the wood.

After wreaking her fury on the immovable wooden beam she suddenly stops in despair with her hands bleeding.

"It is all in vain, Marietjie" Jana says in resignation when she hears Marietjie has stopped trying. She has figured out that it was an earthquake that woke her up this time "You need to leave before another tremor comes".

"I will get you out!" exclaims Marietjie at once, in a tone void of confidence.. She leaves the spot and rushes through the house, trying to find something, ánything she could somehow utilise as an instrument to move the beam or force the door open.

She finds herself in the living room and each step she advances, she hears the breaking sound of the wedding décor covering the entire area under her feet. In her current situation, she doesn't care about these things that seemed to be so important to her before. Her only quest now is opening that door and she is looking for a heavy object to help her break through it. She stumbles over a brass candlestick that also landed on the floor. It was part of her wedding table centerpieces.

"This might just work," Marietjie says to herself, picking up the heavy candlestick and making her way back to the bedroom door.

She hits the wooden beam with the candlestick, she hits the door, she even hits the wall in desperation. Her actions only leave scratches, but there is no real progress. She hits with more fervor, harder and harder, faster and faster and as she is losing the battle and hopes to get Jana out, Marietjie starts screaming in frustration and despair. As an echo to her voice another tremor starts. The shakes are somewhat weaker this time but the fear in Marietjie is growing with every second. Through the dust that is in the air she tries to look into Jana's room and above the rumbling of the earthquake she hears Jana crying.

The overwhelming feeling that she needs to save Jana and the realisation that she is incapable of accomplishing that is too much for Marietjie. She feels despondent, that her heart is going to stop, yet it does not. She is still there, still unable to do anything to free her sister. For a few moments, that feel like hours, she is just standing there, trying to figure out what to do next, sheer panic blocking her from moving.

"I really think you need to leave," says Jana tearfully on the other side of the door between them. Thoughts rush through Marietjie's bewildered mind. She starts to consider leaving the house to get help, but cannot imagine Jana stuck alone in the dark room during the earthquake.

Marietjie does not know how much time has passed before she hears the noise of breaking glass.

"Father?" Marietjie asks with new hope in her voice.

Instead of her father, Marietjie can make out Adriaan's face.

"Marietjie, are you all right?" Adriaan asks.

Marietjie is barely able to speak, she is at the end of her tether, emotional, scared.

"Jana is stuck," she finally utters.

"Where is she?" asks Adriaan.

Marietjie does not answer, she just looks away.

"Marietjie, look at me... Where is Jana?" Marietjie points to the door.

Adriaan tries to push away the wooden beam leaning against the doorpost, and manages to lift it a little. Marietjie is watching him quietly. Adriaan notices how the weight of the beam is cracking the side of the wooden door. He stops and goes over the crack with his hand, assessing something. Then he notices the big brass candlestick.

"Jana, stand back, and do not be afraid! We will get you out" Adriaan says and starts hitting against the door, right on the crack. Bit by bit the crack in the solid door starts widening with every blow with the candlestick. He keeps on hitting the same spot. When the wood splits open further, he sees the door bend under the weight of the building leaning on it. He realises that, if he moves it away completely, the wall might cave in.

"Jana, I need you to try and get through this opening, now," says Adriaan.

Jana manages to squeeze through with much effort.

The moment Jana is free, Marietjie knees fold under her, as if unable to carry the weight of the world any longer. There on the floor she buries her face in her hands and starts crying and shaking uncontrollably.

"We have managed, Marjietjie, Jana is out," says Adriaan in an effort to console her.

"I am all right," confirms Jana, but Marietjie keeps on crying.

Adrian kneels down to hold Marietjie as she cries, then he picks her up and carries her out of the building, careful not to stumble over any object on the floor. Jana follows them.

Marietjie, the strong person that no-one has seen crying before, simply cannot stop.

When they were already safely outside the building, Adriaan says to Marietjie . "Before the earthquake I thought a lot about our fight, but when the earth started to shake beneath my feet, all I could think about was you. I was scared I would lose you."

Marietjie throws her arms around Adriaan and keeps on crying on his chest as he holds her tenderly. It is as if Marietjie is crying to rid her of all the pain, the feelings of despair and inadequacy when she tried to do things right and it did not work out, the loss of her mother (and a great deal of her father) and all other hurtful feelings she has ever had.

> Just then, a car races towards the homestead and stops. Pieter van Schalkwyk jumps out of the car and rushes towards the house. He already knows what has happened in Tulbagh and he is worried sick in his heart about his daughters being in the house and the thoughts of what might or might not have happened to them. Then tears fill his eyes as he comes closer and sees that both Jana and Marietjie are safe and standing outside with Adriaan comforting Marietjie. .

CHAPTER TEN

River Of Lights

As Michael lights a new candle outside of the House, the light chases away the darkness with its playful flame. Every match he strikes sounds almost cheerful – bringing a sense of hope in these uncertain moments. Every candle Antonie hands out, lights up a new face. More and more children appear from the gloom of the night.

When the box of matches is depleted, Michael starts using one of the candles to light up others. Antonie hands out the candles much quicker now, as the kids started lighting them up from each other. In just a few minutes, what seemed to be just a few flickering flames in the dark, becomes a lake of light.

At that point Meneer Arendse and Sollie appear from the doors of the House. Everyone starts cheering, relieved and welcoming them back like heroes. The principal and Sollie are handed their own candles. Meneer Arendse feels in his heart that the earthquake has shaken more things upside down than meets the eye, and has set the scene for some change.

"We are all scared and confused now," says Meneer Arendse. "Though we presume it was an earthquake, we do not know what has really happened and whether it will happen again, but what I can see clearly, is that this night will show who we truly are. In our town there are people that have been hurt tonight, people that are trapped in their houses, people that are alone and terrified. We will go from house to house and will do whatever we can for those who need help. I believe this night will forge our character, and will set the path for our future."

After finishing this important speech, Meneer Arendse then does something that the kids are not used to. Instead of òrdering them, Meneer Arendse ásks the children if they would follow him. He hears a loud cheer of approval and excitement at the prospect following his question. After that, the lake of light turns into a river of light, as the kids follow their principal in an uneven line. This spectacular view of lights moving over the hills and then through the streets of Tulbagh, is fascinating to watch.

Michael is touched by the words of the principal. Perhaps more than anyone, he wants to prove that he is worthy. Instead of going together with the group, Michael asks Antonie not to look for him. Then he goes to the back of the line, blows out his candle and disappears in the dark.

He knows the hillsides like the back of his hand and by the light provided by the fires on the mountains surrounding the town, he speedily makes his way through the torn landscapes, thinking only of Tannie Wilma – that brave, yet vulnerable old lady who lives all alone. She lives on the outskirts of town and does not seem to have any relatives or close friends, so any help might reach her later than anyone else. Michael decides to visit the old woman first and make sure she is alright.

As he approaches the house from the darkness. The front door is locked as expected, so he walks around the building to look for a way in. The side window is broken, glass is shattered on the ground and he climbs in carefully, avoiding being cut by the broken glass. To his surprise the building on the inside looks nothing like on the outside. Even though the earthquake has visibly damaged and displaced almost everything, it still seems a cosy place.

The moon is beaming through the broken windows lighting Michael's path. As he slowly walks through the room, he sees the photos of a much younger Wilma, then a photo of Wilma in her wedding dress next to her husband. Michael does not have time to dig into Wilma's past, so he keeps on walking till he sees Wilma sitting in her old armchair, covered with dust.

"Tannie Wilma?" calls Michael.

"What are you doing here?" asks Tannie Wilma in a stern, angry tone.

"We are helping people in need Tannie, and I came to help you," replies Michael.

"I do not need any help. Get out of here," says Tannie Wilma, this time with indifference.

"Tannie Wilma, it is not safe here. You need to leave the house," Michael tries to persuade her.

"This is my home and I am not leaving," says Wilma decidedly.

For a minute Michael is not sure what to say. Then he moves uncomfortably close to Wilma and states, "If you do not leave the house, neither will I. So I will just stand here, irritating you."

"How dare you!" Wilma starts screaming at Michael, but she is interrupted by a new tremor. Almost immediately the heavy wooden cupboard filled with crockery and cutlery starts shaking, one of its legs cracks and it falls over toward them. Both Michael and Wilma scream, but their voices drown in the loud roar of the tremor.

When the tremor ceases, Wilma sees her broken glassware and China scattered across the room. Then she notices Michael. Something is strange about the way he is lying. Maybe he was trying to protect himself and Wilma from the falling cupboard and reached out with his hand in a futile attempt to stop it, maybe it has happened differently, but the fact is Michael's arm is stuck under the fallen cupboard.

Tannie Wilma tries to push away the heavy piece of furniture. She quickly realizes that, even if she was a much younger woman, she would not have been able to lift this solid piece of heavy wood. Without any delay or second thoughts, Wilma leaves moaning

Michael on the floor and rushes out to get some help.

PART THREE

CHAPTER ONE

Aftermath

The Tulbagh earthquake was the most destructive in South African history, registering an alarming 6.3 on the Richter scale. During the 15 seconds, twelve people lost their lives, and more were injured. The main shock was followed by a series of aftershocks over an extended period of the time. The largest aftershock occurred only the next year and had a magnitude of 5.7.

The Tulbagh earthquake itself brought widespread damage not only to Tulbagh, being the centre of it, but also to the towns of Ceres and Wolseley. It was caused by the ground shifting of 20cm over 20km. This destructive force of nature was named Gertruda, but went down in history as the Tulbagh earthquake.

Gertruda unrooted Tulbagh's favourite tree, Uncle Tom. It destroyed or damaged most of the buildings in

Tulbagh. It painted cracks on the roads, ruptured pipes and toppled gravestones. The walls of some dams cracked, but fortunately have not failed. The landslide blocked the Tulbagh Kloof pass and cut off the town. Gertruda caused fires on the mountains that were a great threat for the farms in the vicinity.

The night of the earthquake passed and when the sun lit the valley the next morning, nothing seemed the same. It was as if walls, both physical and imaginary, were shattered. The dust covered everyone's face and took away all the differences in skin colour. That morning they were all just survivors. The earthquake did not just turn the town upside down, it also brought people closer.

Later that day the army arrived. They brought tents and set them up where there was enough space: on rugby fields, on school grounds. Half of the population of Tulbagh were left homeless, and so they stayed in tents for months, while their houses were being restored or even rebuilt completely. People from the neighbouring communities provided them with food, clothes, blankets.

The morning after the earthquake, Ben and Truia were back at their old farmhouse. What stood strong for so many years was shaken in one night beyond recognition. Ben was inspecting the house he grew up in, possessions and sentiments that came with thirty years of married life, furniture that he had inherited from his grandfathers and great grandfathers were damaged – some beyond repair. There was a lot of work to be done. Fortunately Hanri decided to stay in Tulbagh until he and his father could repair most of the damage caused by the earthquake.

Karla left for Cape Town with her suitcase, that she had retrieved from the damaged house of Truia and Ben. She was really anxious that the news of the earthquake could reach her parents, so she phoned them as soon as she could. She booked a room in the hotel in Cape Town and left on the first available flight to the Netherlands. By that time Karla had no doubt that her real home was back in the Netherlands and she was glad to return there.

Sadly, little Sune's house was seriously damaged. Isak, Sune and the rest of their family had to live in a tent for almost a year. They built a storage shack next to the tent to safekeep some possessions retrieved from the damaged house. until a new house could be erected for them.

Grace's house survived, it suffered minimal damage. She was grateful to God for saving her home and almost immediately, invited one of the instantly homeless families to stay with her.

The night of the earthquake Michael had to wait for Tannie Wilma to get help. By the time he was rescued from under the antique cupboard, it was too late to save his arm. Tannie Wilma visited him in hospital after the amputation and brought him fruit from her garden.

The orphanage house, built in 1843, had collapsed and all the children were sent to another children's establishment in the town of Somerset West. Their former House was later restored and used as a library.

Marietjie felt that the earthquake shook off a great deal of emotional weight she had been carrying. With the love of her father, sister and Adriaan she finally started recovering from the loss of her mother.

Marietjie and Adriaan got married in an outside ceremony just a month after the earthquake. They brought out a few tables and invited close friends and relatives for a modest reception. Jana did not have to play the role of a flower girl after all, but Marietjie did request her to wear a decent dress. Marietjie and Adriaan had a perfectly imperfect small wedding.

The morning after the earthquake the whole Republic of South Africa was reading about this natural disaster in newspapers. Tulbagh became famous instantly . The town drew many people: those who wanted to help and those who were curious to see the consequences of an earthquake.

One of the first things people saw in Tulbagh was Church Street, a central point of this agricultural town. Church street that boasted charming 18th and 19th century houses in Cape Dutch, Victorian and Edwardian styles, now lay in ruins.

The decision was made to restore the whole street, a colossal project for everyone involved. The architects used a drawing made in 1811 for restoration work.

Each house in Church street was unique, but they were all united by common elements, as if different pieces of one mosaic. The street, with blue mountains in the background, became a symbol of a quiet South African town.

Through the whole process of restoration Tulbagh was drawing visitors. A small farming community gave way to a bustling tourist town. To this day people come to Tulbagh and visit its museum (the Dutch Reformed Church at the time of the disaster) to find out more about the earthquake.

29 SEPTEMBER 2019

The wine tours are a popular pastime in the picturesque country of South Africa.

Tourists and locals alike enjoy visiting wine farms scattered all over the country. They appreciate stunning views of valleys and mountains drowning in the warm bright sun. They have relaxed conversations while tasting unique and rich South African wines.

In the valley of Tulbagh surrounded by mountains on both sides, the wine tasting groups can travel between farms on the horse backs. The sound of the horses walking between the vineyards breaks the quiet sound of the valley. The animals are so tame and so used to touring the guests that even people without experience can ride them.

Today's group are mostly tourists excited for a horseback adventure. The valleys and mountains are fresh with a morning breather and warm with the rising sun. It is easy to dissolve in this magical setting forgetting where you came from or where you are going.

The tour guide, a strong man with a gray beard, a warm smile and a prosthetic arm, is taking a tour group to the mountain side, to see the whole town of Tulbagh from above. While tourists are taking photos trying to fit in both their faces and the view, he is taking a few moments to gaze down. This view is special to him and the town beneath is so much more than a sleeping tourist attraction. He is trying to find something important beneath, something that is not there anymore. He wants to see the town as it used to be many years ago.

The tour guide's name is Michael Carelse and he is looking into his past, the time when he was happy, despite the circumstances.

WHAT PEOPLE AGAINST RACE CLASSIFICATION (PARC) IS:

PARC is a civil rights activist group that opposes the referencing of the South African population in terms of race groupings. They deny race identities. Humans are not defined by the colour of their skin, but by the content of their character. There exists only one race and that is the human race. They encourage people to not refer to themselves or to others as Coloured people, Black people, Indian people or White people, but just as people and first and foremost, South Africans. Because of the negative stereotyping that is linked to racial categories, we want to do away with such terminologies in our society. For example, if you say someone is white, you might say he is superior, if you say someone is black, you might say he is inferior, if you say someone is Coloured, you might say he is confused and mixed, and if you say someone is an Indian, you might say he doesn't belong here. We don't believe in a rainbow nation, we believe in a nation. We strive for a change in the South African constitution so that the referencing and collection of racial data could be stopped by state law. We dream that we all could one day live in a country that is free from race classification requirements and people referring to others by race. That the "they" would become "we". Through education and reconciliation we try to bring people together so that all our people could unashamedly stand under one national flag, as South Africans. We demonstrate what we believe in through our PARC T-shirts with the wording on it that reads: "I'm not a Coloured, Black, Indian or White person. I am a SOUTH AFRICAN.

HOW CAN YOU HELP / GET INVOLVED / ACTION STEPS

1. Educate yourself on racial matters.
2. Reject the cultural referencing of your racial lineage. Proclaim that you are a South African, first.
3. Visit our website (www.parcsa.co.za) and spread the information pamphlet about PARC.
4. Wear our PARC T-shirts with the wording on it: I'm not a Coloured, Black, Indian or White person. I am a SOUTH AFRICAN.
5. Sign our PARC petition form.
6. Refuse to fill in race classification details on any form that requires it.
7. Support our plea to the Constitutional Court of South Africa to change race-based laws.
8. Do not feel hurt, or bothered, if someone calls you a racist. Instead, play the PARC songs.
9. Give acknowledgement and credit for positive mending of racial relationships in our society what you became aware of.
10. Enjoy and learn from our PARC posters, songs, articles, books, preferred movies, radio debates and join our T-shirt demonstrations.

www.ingramcontent.com/pod-product-compliance
Lightning Source LLC
Chambersburg PA
CBHW072203100526
44589CB00015B/2346